DUNMORA

The story of a heritage manor house on Vancouver Island

By
Valerie Green

ISBN 978-0-88839-005-9 [trade hardcover]
ISBN 978-0-88839-008-0 [trade softcover]

Library & Archives Canada Cataloguing in Publication

Green, Valerie -, author
Dunmora : the story of a heritage manor house on Vancouver Island / Valerie Green.
ISBN 978-0-88839-005-9 (hardcover).--ISBN 978-0-88839-008-0 (softcover)
1. Dunmora (B.C.). 2. Historic buildings--British Columbia--Saanich Peninsula. 3. Dwellings--British Columbia--Saanich Peninsula--History. 4. Saanich Peninsula (B.C.)--History. 5. Saanich Peninsula (B.C.)--Biography. I. Title.
FC3845.S23Z535 2017 971.11'28 C2017-904493-1

Printed in Canada— Friesens

Editor: T. Laviolette
Production: D. Williams, M. Lamont
Cover Design: M. Lamont

We acknowledge the financial support of the Government of Canada through the Book Publishing Industry Development Program (BPIDP) for our publishing activities.

Published simultaneously in Canada and the United States by

HANCOCK HOUSE PUBLISHERS, LTD

19313 Zero Ave, Surrey, BC V3Z 9R9 Canada
(604) 538-1114 Fax (604) 538-2262

HANCOCK HOUSE PUBLISHERS

#104- 4550 Birch Bay-Lynden Rd, Blaine, WA U.S.A 98230-9436
(800) 938-1114 Fax (800) 983-2262
www.hancockhouse.com sales@hancockhouse.com

"A house is made of walls and beams; a home is built with love and dreams."

— Author unknown

Dedicated

To Gerald and Léonie May who created the legacy.

Dunmora, shown here in 1955

Table of Contents

Aerial view of Dunmora – Jan 19, 1945,

Chapter 1: In The Beginning...

The pioneer, the architect and the builder

THE STORY OF any house typically begins long before it is actually built. It originates with the land on which the house will eventually be erected.

So the story of Dunmora, originally with an address on McPhail Road on the peninsula of Vancouver Island, British Columbia, Canada, really starts long before 1921 when Gerald Henderson May and his wife Léonie purchased the land on which they intended to build their first family home.

The land and its surroundings had for centuries been home to the Coast Salish First Nations people. Long before the area was cleared by early white pioneers in order to farm, the First Nations had walked the narrow trails through dense forest land where they hunted for deer or headed down to the water's edge to fish. The natural flora of the region included forests of Douglas fir, Western red cedar, arbutus, Garry Oak and hemlock.

All that changed drastically in the 1850s when James Douglas of the Hudson's Bay Company (HBC) purchased North and South Saanich from the native people. In fact, between 1850 and 1854, James Douglas signed fourteen treaties with First Nations communities on Vancouver Island, dealing with areas from Victoria to Sooke, out to the Saanich Peninsula and in Nanaimo. According to those treaties, "the Indigenous chiefs and their communities agreed to surrender, entirely and for ever," most of their territories to the Hudson's Bay Company. [1]

By 1858 the land was already being surveyed to prepare for settlement. Early white settlers soon started to arrive and a new era began.

1 Cole Harris, Making Native Space: Colonialism, Resistance, and Reserves in British Columbia, p. 19.

Welcome to Dunmora, as it appears today.

Many of the early settlers on the peninsula were of British descent. They immediately cleared the land in order to pursue resource-based economic activities such as logging, fishing and agriculture. The soil was perfect for agricultural activities.

One of the first of those early settlers was Angus (Aeneas) McPhail whose name today graces the road on which Dunmora originally stood. McPhail was born in the Orkney Islands in Scotland in 1809 and grew up speaking Gaelic. He had signed on with the HBC as a young man in 1837 and soon afterwards left Scotland for the New World sailing aboard the *Prince Rupert.* After spending a year in the Red River District of Canada he headed west. He arrived at Fort Langley in 1838 and while there married a Cree woman 'in the custom of the country' (this was a simple ceremony performed between white men and native women without benefit of clergy). They had one daughter, Anne, but tragically his wife died in childbirth.

By 1846, McPhail had moved to Vancouver Island and was stationed at Fort Victoria where he operated a dairy farm on the outskirts of the Fort. The farm was said to produce the finest milk and butter around. He remarried in June of 1851 and in 1855 headed out to the Saanich Inlet on the peninsula of Vancouver Island where he staked out 177 acres and built a cabin. This rich, fertile land near the west end of Mount Newton Cross Road was ideal for farming. McPhail had worked hard clearing the trees and cutting shingles for his cabin, which would eventually be called Bay Farm. It was in that cabin that his second wife gave birth to another daughter, Marie, in 1859. That same year McPhail received pre-emption papers from the HBC for his property and he became the official owner of all the land he had staked out and on which he had been squatting for four years.

McPhail had sold some of his property in 1855 to Peter Lind, a hotel entrepreneur who built a hotel on the southwest corner of Mount Newton Cross Road and West Saanich, now long since demolished. The remainder of his land McPhail eventually sold to Alphonse Verdier, who had by then married his sixteen-year-old daughter, Anne. Tragedy struck again when McPhail's second wife died and soon afterwards he left the peninsula with his young daughter, Marie, and moved to the Cowichan district up-island where she was cared for by the Sisters of St. Ann.

In the early 1870s, McPhail moved back to Central Saanich and farmed for a while with George Stelly, another Saanich peninsula pioneer. Five years later, daughter Marie McPhail married Frank Gravelle, the son of an HBC man.

It was rumoured that McPhail ended his days in an Old Men's Home in Victoria where he died in 1884. He is buried in the Roman Catholic section of Ross Bay Cemetery, but his name is still fondly remembered by his many descendants on the peninsula and is, of course, perpetuated in the road leading to Dunmora.

By 1921, sixty acres of that original Saanich Inlet land were owned by a Mr. Pichon, a Frenchman who ran a hunting/fishing business in Victoria. He also kept a log cabin on his land in Central Saanich which he frequented on occasion when he simply wanted to get away and enjoy the wilderness life in order to hunt and fish.

The Pichon log house, where the Mays spent part of their time while Dunmora was built.

There was nearby granite quarry that in the early part of the twentieth century was the big attraction for those who wanted to buy Pichon's land. It was said that an interested party wanted to make the quarry workable again using the granite to build Ogden Point[2] on Dallas Road in Victoria.

2 The two piers for the Odgen Point breakwater eventually were built 1914–1916, and constructed of concrete blocks and concrete on a rock base. The piers and a cargo warehouse were all completed in 1918. MacFarlane, John M. & Murray P. Polson. 2012. "The Ogden Point Breakwater, Victoria, BC." Nauticapedia.ca/piers and a cargo warehouse were all completed in 1918. MacFarlane, John M. & Murray P. Polson. 2012. "The Ogden Point Breakwater, Victoria, BC." Nauticapedia.ca/

No one, other than the Mays had wanted the Pichon land in order to simply build a home.

In early 1921 Pichon decided to sell those sixty acres and the cabin to Gerald and Léonie May. In later years the log cabin was to prove a small bone of contention with future owners of Dunmora. Access to it actually went through nearby land attached to the Point Colville house next door and this easement was not released until much later.

By the early summer of 1921, the princely sum of $12,468 (amounting to approximately $200 per acre) had passed hands between the Mays and Mr. Pichon for the land. This was a significant amount of money in the 1920s and the expenses for building and furnishing the house, of course, had not even begun.

The Mays wanted to build their home on this spectacular piece of property from the moment they first stood high up on the bluff and overlooked the beautiful Saanich inlet in 1921. They had been entranced by those surroundings and made a quick decision to buy. In order to build the kind of fine home they envisioned, however, both an exceptional architect and a first-class building contractor were needed.

The man they chose to design their home was well-known architect of the day, John Malcolm Charles Keith. Recalling Mr. Keith, on a tape recording made by her grandson Trevor May in 1992, Léonie May described him as "a rather ordinary, unimposing fellow" and stated that she had to alter some of his initial plans because the house was placed too high on the bluff. "However, all in all he did a good job though," she added. The Mays knew exactly what they wanted in their home and all these requirements were relayed to Keith. Working together, these architectural blueprints included many visionary aspects such as ensuite bathrooms attached to each bedroom, something that was not often seen in 1920 home architecture. The rooms were also far larger than was the norm. Dunmora was designed with many rooms in the English Tudor-style with the appearance of a magnificent estate surrounded by delightful grounds.

Architect John Keith was born in Nairn, Scotland in 1858. He was the son of a clergyman and this probably accounted for the many churches he later designed throughout Greater Victoria. He was educated in various grammar schools throughout England and then joined the architectural practice

Construction in 1922 on the entrance front.

West Corner under construction in 1922.

of a Scottish architect, Alexander Ross, who had designed the cathedral in Inverness. Keith later returned to London, but in 1887 decided to immigrate to California where he practiced for two years before moving north to Seattle.

In 1891 he came to Victoria, British Columbia in order to enter a competition to design Christ Church Cathedral and the Memorial Hall. He easily won that competition, a win which would earn him fellowship into the Royal Institute of British Columbia Architects. However, the Memorial Hall was not built until 1923 and the cathedral itself not until 1926. Nonetheless, this prestigious start in his architectural vocation in Victoria earned him much attention and led to a fifty-year career in the city and throughout Vancouver Island.

During those years, he designed many homes in Greater Victoria as well as Anglican churches in Nanaimo and Port Alberni. In 1925, he also drew up the original plans for St. George the Martyr Church on St. George's Lane in Cadboro Bay, but the church was not built at that time. His plans were, however, revised and used to build the church in the 1950s. Keith also designed the old Saanich Municipal Hall on West Saanich Road in 1911, St. Martin-in-the-Fields Anglican Church on Obed Avenue in 1926, the Moss Street

School, the Seaman's Institute in James Bay, the old City Police Court building on Fisgard Street and the Chapel in the Royal Jubilee Hospital. He died on his birthday, December 19, in 1940 at the age of eighty-two.

The building contractor chosen by the Mays was David Walter Burnett (1883–1960) whose offices were located at the corner of Fort and Langley Streets in Victoria. That building is no longer there and a parking lot now occupies the site.

D.W. Burnett Contracting was a well-known building firm in Victoria from the early part of the century. The company had worked on many buildings in the area, including being the main contractors for the building of the Empress Hotel as well as some subsequent additions and renovations, and The Royal Oak Inn (later the Thatch and now the popular Fireside Grill Restaurant) on West Saanich Road. David Walter Burnett was in fact the co-owner of The Royal Oak Inn with Vera Hannah Levy, and the site they chose in 1939 was at a strategic intersection of roads which led to the new airport at that time and to the Butchart Gardens. The inn was designed by architect Hubert Savage and, according to Burnett's great-granddaughter Karen Burnett McLeod, the original thatched roof used for the building was shipped from England. Unfortunately the business did not survive for long due to the outbreak of World War II when many such businesses failed. Later, the building became the Maltwood Museum owned by the Maltwood family who donated the museum to the University of Victoria. In 1980 the university sold the property to the Saanich municipality. Architect Bradley Shuya redesigned the interior and exterior restorations which were completed in the year 2000, enabling the building to become a restaurant. It still retains the Arts and Crafts/Tudor styles favoured by Burnett.

For many years D.W. Burnett Contracting entered a float in the Victoria Day Parade on which rode Burnett's only granddaughter, always so proud of her granddad. When D.W. Burnett finally retired, the company was renamed The Island Building Supply.

Above: Builder David Walter Burnett

Many of the attributes and building techniques favoured by Burnett are present in Dunmora: the Tudor style, the elegant bedrooms, bathrooms, wood paneling and beams throughout, all contrasting with the use of granite taken from the quarry on the property. The wooden floors were constructed of edge-grain fir and not hardwood like today and the excellent quality of those floors needed regular waxing through the years. The leaded casement windows used on the second floor were shipped from England and believed to have come from a church. They all have decorative wrought-iron fasteners. The only thing the house initially lacked was any kind of insulation, but it did have a built-in fire safety system.

Building contractors who have worked on the house in various stages of restoration and renovation through the years have all highly praised the original workmanship of D.W. Burnett who, like architect John Keith, had an incredible futuristic vision when working on Dunmora.

The house was to become so well known in the area that for many years any mail sent to the May family could simply be addressed as "Dunmora," Turgoose Bay, Vancouver Island, Canada, and it would always reach its destination. Turgoose Bay was named for pioneer William Turgoose whose son, Fred Turgoose, operated a small post office called "Turgoose" from his farmhouse across the East Saanich Road. Later, Dunmora's postal address became "Dunmora," Saanichton, Vancouver Island, BC. Today, as a result of the surrounding Dunmora Estates subdivision, the postal address is 480 Dunmora Court.

In recent decades, residential and commercial development has become widespread on the Saanich peninsula, but there are still many wilderness parks, the largest being Gowlland Tod Provincial Park. Today the peninsula is also home to the oldest agricultural exhibition in Western Canada, the Saanich Fair, which is sponsored by the North and South Saanich Agricultural Society and takes place in early September every year.

Once the plans were drawn up and the building had begun to take shape, Gerald and Léonie May were anxious to settle in with their family and make Dunmora the warm, intimate household they envisioned.

Chapter 2: The May Family History...

Before Dunmora

Gerald Henderson May, Dunmora's first owner, was born on January 7, 1888 in Honolulu, Hawaii when it was still the Kingdom of Hawaii. He was the son of Thomas (Tom) May (born 1850) and Julia Wight (born 1853) and was already more than familiar with a life of wealth and privilege. His father had been the recipient of most of his Uncle Henry's estate.

Henry May had owned a well-known coffee roasting and import grocery company in Honolulu known as Henry May & Company. When Henry died of malaria on October 1, 1884[3] with no offspring, he left most of his estate to his oldest nephew, Tom. He also left $5,000 to be used for the building of a church in Honolulu and $10,000 for a niece, Kate May, to be invested by trustees for her in the business of Henry May & Co. until she reached the age of twenty-eight. He left his house and all household goods to another niece, Betsey Ann, who was married to a British Naval Lieutenant. Several siblings and other nieces and nephews also shared in his considerable estate.[4]

Tom and Julia May had five children; four boys, Arthur, James Percy, Gerald and Cyril and one girl, Vera. The children were all privately tutored until age twelve and then sent to England for further

3 Daily Pacific Commercial Advertiser, Honolulu, Oct. 17th, 1884.

4 Will of Henry May, dated 18 June, 1880, Nottinghamshire Archives, Administered 20 Feb, 1891

The front entrance in July, 1922.

education. In 1907, at the age of nineteen, Gerald May attended Cambridge University from where he eventually graduated in civil engineering. By then the whole family had moved to Bournemouth in England because Julia was taken ill and could no longer live in a tropical climate.

After Tom's death from arterial sclerosis in 1910, followed shortly thereafter by Julia's death from throat cancer, the family money was divided among their five offspring. Gerald especially was devastated by his mother's death as they had been very close.

After finally completing his degree, Gerald was undecided about what to do next. By then, World War I had begun, but due to a serious lung health issue (pneumothorax) Gerald was declared unfit for service. One day while walking around in London, he was handed a white feather by a woman who was a member of the White Feather Movement, a propaganda organization campaigning young, outwardly fit young men to enlist in the army.

The white feathers were a symbol of cowardice and were distributed by women of the Order of the White Feather to any man they saw who seemed capable of joining the forces but was still not wearing a uniform to signify he was fighting for his country. The idea was to shame these men by showing them how they were viewed by women. Many were indeed intimidated and were persuaded to join the army immediately.

For Gerald it was a devastating experience; he was upset and ashamed even though he had a legitimate reason for not being able to fight for his country because of his respiratory condition. Later, against doctor's orders, he did try to learn to fly, but in the process almost lost his life when one of his lungs collapsed. It was a miracle he survived. The side effects of this health issue remained with him for the rest of his life.

Once the war was over, Gerald travelled for a while trying to decide his future. He returned to Waikiki for a while, but in 1920 he came back to England and stayed at the Oatlands Park Hotel near Weybridge. It was while staying there that he met Léonie Fredericks, a young woman he had first seen in 1913 at the wedding of her sister Melita to his brother Cyril. At that time Léonie had only been twelve years old and Gerald many years her senior. In 1920, however, when he met her for the second time, she was nineteen and he became smitten by her beauty and intelligence. It

The veranda front soon after construction in July, 1922.

was love at first sight for them both. They were engaged soon afterwards in Switzerland and in March of 1921, following Léonie`s twentieth birthday, they were married in a London church. Gerald waited until she had just turned twenty because he later said, "I did not want to be accused of marrying a teenager and robbing the cradle." The Mays spent their honeymoon in Lynmouth in Devon.

Léonie was the daughter of Alexander (Rex) William Friedrichs (later changed to Fredericks) and Elizabeth (Bessie) Sheppard. She was well-educated, having attended the prestigious Roedean School for girls aged eleven to eighteen on the outskirts of Brighton, East Sussex, in England, and came from an equally well-off family as her new husband.

Her father was German by birth (born in Bavaria). At the turn of the century, when he was just eighteen, he met and fell in love with Bessie Sheppard and had come to England to work. When World War I broke out many years later, Rex was still not naturalized English, so was immediately detained in a prison camp.

Family history states that Bessie's mother called in a favour with Prime Minister Lloyd George, and Rex was allowed to return to his home and stay within a one-mile radius of it until such time as the house sold, whereupon he had to remove himself and his family from the country. Having previously worked in Argentina from about 1907 to 1911 as a brewery manager, he chose to return to that country and eventually was made an Argentine citizen courtesy of an influential Argentine friend named Kintana. Rex did well for his family while in Argentina by speculating successfully in real estate. Later, they moved to the Claremont Hotel in Berkeley, California, and eventually to Canada.

While on their honeymoon in Lynmouth, Gerald and Léonie May made a decision that would change the rest of their lives. As they sat on the beach one day Gerald asked his new bride where in the world she would like to live. She knew she would be happy with him anywhere so when he suggested Victoria on Vancouver Island in Canada, she readily agreed. Gerald remembered Victoria from having stopped there during his school years travelling back and forth between Hawaii and the United Kingdom.

Having made their decision to move to Canada, the Mays immediately set off on their adventure, travelling aboard the *RMS Empress of France* across the Atlantic and then by train across Canada to Victoria. They stayed first at the Empress Hotel and later in a cottage on Chamberlain Street in Oak Bay. Once they had purchased their land on the peninsula they moved into the Brentwood Hotel (then the Brentwood College) while their house was being built. They also spent days at the nearby Pichon log cabin to watch the building progress.

It was an exciting time for the Mays. Their waterfront estate would turn out to be a well-known landmark in the area. Set among woodlands of conifers, arbutus and Garry oaks overlooking the Saanich Inlet, Dunmora was very distinctive and could be seen for miles around because of its original red roof and tall granite chimneys. The roof was made of wooden shingles painted with a copper-based paint that was applied every decade. It lasted approximately eighty years before it had to be replaced!

The only nearby neighbour was Point Colville house, which was painted a bright yellow with green trim. It was built in 1912 as a country house for Viscount Colville. It had been shipped to that site from the prairies as a Sears pre-built house and erected on the rocks opposite to Henderson point. Various members of the Colville family lived there in the early years until the eldest son, Alick, inherited his father's title and estate in the early 1920s and had to return to Scotland.

A later owner of Point Colville was Mrs. Emily Johnstone who during the 1950s and early 1960s had a caretaker named Melville Rysdale TenBroeke living in a cottage in the forest at number 8074. He was an interesting English gentleman who had moved to Canada before World War I and joined the Canadian forces. He was commander of the No. 2 Company of the Princess Patricia's Canadian Light Infantry (PPCLI) during World War I and was instrumental in the capture of Vimy Ridge. After the war, TenBroeke was requested to head up a Royal Guard of Honour at the wedding ceremony of Princess Patricia of Connaught on February 27, 1919. He became a good friend of both the May family and the Simpson family, who were later owners of Dunmora. He died on May 3, 1963.

For many years both the Dunmora and Point Colville houses could be clearly seen for miles across the inlet from the Malahat highway. Passing boats in the inlet also used the houses as marker points—the red roof of Dunmora and the bright yellow and green paint of Point Colville.

Gerald, Léonie, Moira and baby Peter, Christmas 1924.

Beyond their close proximity, the histories of the two houses also became intertwined over the years.

Chapter 3: The Early May Years (1921–1939)

"The Fair Mistress of Dunmora"

By July 1921 the site for the house was already being cleared and things were moving ahead at a steady pace. Decisions were made quickly by the Mays and in November that year the foundation was already being poured.

The speed with which the workers were building was quite incredible because by February of 1922, May family photographs show that the ground floor was already completely in place. This floor would include three fireplaces, a stove in the kitchen and a furnace in the basement. In March they were planning the master suite on the second floor and by April the second floor was already fully framed. The west corner of the house was completed by May and in June the half-timbering and roof were well underway.

During all these proceedings, Léonie became pregnant with twins. The Mays were still living in the small cottage on Chamberlain Street so that Léonie would be near the Jubilee Hospital. However, in Gerald's ledger books various payments are noted to a Victoria private hospital. Sadly, one twin did not survive the birth, leaving only their beautiful daughter Moira, who was born healthy. She arrived in June 1922, and on August 22 a family album photograph shows a happy group of family and friends celebrating Moira's christening party on the lawn at Dunmora.[5]

5 May Family Archives Collection. Photo Albums. Léonie May.

For many years, passing boats in the inlet used the red roof of Dunmora and the bright yellow and green paint of neighboring Point Colville to navigate.

The view from the dining room into the living room of Dunmora, circa 1923.

The dining room of Dunmora,. circa 1923.

An interesting collection of photographs in the May family archives reveals those first years and those to follow in pictorial form mainly because of Léonie's hobby of meticulous record keeping of photographic images. She also developed her own photographs in a darkroom in the house. Like her husband Gerald, who kept equally intricate details in his numerous ledgers of money being spent and coming in during those years, Léonie kept photographs of family events accurately and painstakingly in several albums which have survived for almost a century.

Gerald's ledgers include his banking with the Westminster Bank in London and the Canadian Bank of Commerce and, of special interest, are notations of all the furniture purchased to decorate the interior of Dunmora. The items are listed by room, such as: Lounge, Smoking Room, Dining Room, Sunroom, Veranda and even Pantry. The upstairs items include furniture for the Master Bedroom, Spare Bedrooms and Moira's Room, plus Dressing Rooms and Nursery. A Persian rug, for example, cost $650, a chesterfield (sofa) and two armchairs $367.63, a writing desk was $69.50 and a baby grand piano $1,000.[6]

6 Gerald May Ledgers, May Family Archives Collection.

The Dunmora living room looking toward the fireplace seating area, circa 1923.

Sunlight pours into the living room of Dunmora, circa 1923.

In the smoking room, $45 was spent on a carved oak table and curtains cost $52.49. Various candlesticks, lamp shades, desk lamps and leather cushions are also listed in the ledgers. The dining-room suite consisting of a table, six chairs, a sideboard and display cabinet cost $810.50.[7]

All these items for the house were purchased from downtown stores such as Spencers, Weilers and the Hudson's Bay Company and, knowing the Mays' penchant for only the best, they would have been excellent pieces of the day.

In addition to the family's personal household expenses were, of course, the fees that had already been paid to architect Keith and the builders, D.W. Burnett and crew. No expense was spared in the grandeur that would become their home for the next forty years. Gerald wrote in his ledgers on a daily basis as he sat in the inglenook in his smoking room/study to the left of the front hallway. A second inglenook was built to the right of the entrance. Evidence from these ledgers also show that Gerald May played the stock market in a modest way, perhaps to help expand his income.

7 Ibid.

Soon after the May family moved into their house during the latter part of 1922, a nearby neighbour told Léonie that she didn't believe she would last there for more than a year because she was a "city girl at heart" and would not enjoy the total isolation of rural Saanich. That neighbour was, of course, proved totally wrong. Not only did Léonie survive their first very cold winter at the house, with at least three feet of snow underfoot, but the Mays stayed in their house for forty years, moving only because of Gerald's poor health in 1961 and eventual death in August of 1962. Léonie herself stayed on the other half of the property in another smaller version of Dunmora (named New Dunmora) until the year 1972, eventually spending her last years in a house on Salmon Road in Central Saanich which she named Dunevan after her childhood home in Weybridge.

In those early years, Léonie always maintained she was never lonely despite the remoteness of Dunmora. The house was most definitely secluded from the outside world, but Léonie owned her own car so was able to travel into town whenever she needed to, and they frequently entertained visitors, including her parents who often stayed with them. Eventually her parents moved to nearby North Saanich to a house they called La Quinta, so Léonie never felt lonely. She also had a loving husband and her children to fill her days. Following Moira's birth in 1922, a son, Peter, arrived in March of 1924 followed by another son, Ian, in August of 1925. Ian was actually born *in* Dunmora and, to date, appears to be the only person ever born in the house.

The house was secluded, but Léonie owned her own car, shown here in 1932, so was able to travel into town whenever she needed.

That same year a serendipitous event occurred that affected the naming of their home. The Mays had initially decided upon the name Dunmoa, which was a combination of places they had come from: Dunevan was the name of Léonie's home in England, and Manoa was the childhood home of Gerald in Honolulu. However, that name was not meant to be.

Captain Sinclair, a neighbour who lived on Lawrence Road a little further down West Saanich Road, visited them one day bringing a gift which was destined to change the name of their house. Captain Sinclair was originally from the prairies and had told them that as a child he had been exposed to particularly severe winter weather one year causing frostbite to both his ears and leaving him totally deaf. Although he was hard to converse with, he did enjoy writing poetry and on that particular day he brought one of his poems for the Mays. He had called it "The Fair Mistress of Dunmora" to honour Léonie, the new lady of the manor. The Mays were enchanted with the name and decided to keep it for their house. Thus the name Dunmora was born.

Many Chinese labourers had worked on the building of Dunmora and one named Sam remained after the other workers had left. "We just sort of inherited him," recalled Léonie in the tape recording she made with her grandson Trevor. "He came to the door one day and simply said 'you want cook?' I told him that I would indeed need a cook and he replied, 'I will come,' and then he just started walking away without telling us what he wanted to be paid. He seemed to like us and wanted to stay on but we had no idea

Sam taking care of Moira May in the 1920s.

what to pay him or what the going wage rate was for Chinese workers, so we consulted with people at Government House to see what their servants were paid. We then paid Sam the same. He stayed with us for about ten years and then returned to China to die, a custom many Chinese followed."

Léonie also recalled memories of some of her first neighbours. One lady in particular, a Mrs. Coldwell, was a memorable woman. She kept some Jersey cows on her land from which she produced delicious Devonshire cream. One of the Chinese servants would walk over every day to bring back bottles of milk for the May family, or the nanny would walk the children up there for exercise. Mrs. Coldwell never left her house and always seemed to have some milk boiling on the back of the stove to make the Devonshire cream, which she would dole out to the children with an old spoon. When you visited her (according to Léonie who claimed she was a real talker and nicknamed her the village gossip) she especially enjoyed telling people about the work she did "laying out dead people" to make them look presentable for viewing.

"Eventually she passed away," recalled Léonie, and, "being Roman Catholic she was also 'laid out' herself for viewing. It was the first funeral I had ever attended and I vividly remember her face being all rouged up. She looked so different in death and not a bit as I remembered her. In fact she looked quite grotesque!"

Mrs. Caldwell, the Village Gossip.

Running a house as large as Dunmora and raising their three children during the 1920s and 1930s obviously meant that Léonie needed some domestic help. In addition to Sam, the Mays hired a succession of Chinese servants through the years and, by all accounts, all were kind, faithful, hard-working people

Bing carrying boys in a basket in 1931.

who took good care of them all. Their stories are collectively told here.

Sam, for instance, became a man of many talents and was much beloved by the family. He took great care of them all as cook, as well as taking care of the children for whom he held an especially soft spot in his heart. In the winter he would wake up at two o'clock every morning in order to stoke the furnace to make sure the children were always warm. Without insulation, the house was obviously very cold with the only heat coming from the furnace or the many fireplaces.The only source of heat for the servants' quarters over the garage came from a water pipe that travelled above ground along the trellis past the kitchen garden to heat a radiator. One day, Léonie noticed that Bing, another Chinese servant, wore a coat that smelled musty and it dawned on her how cold and damp the accommodation over the garage must be. She and Gerald then had electric heat installed to remedy the problem. But neither Sam nor Bing had ever complained.

Chew, a servant for the Mays, shown in the kitchen in 1955.

The day that Sam left for China to die many years later, Léonie summoned him to her bedroom where she was recuperating from a broken collar bone after a fall from her horse. She presented him with an album of memories in gratitude for his service; Sam was apparently reduced to tears.

A three-tiered cake in the shape of a pagoda that Bing baked for the family.

Another Chinese houseboy often wrote poetry for Léonie. "None of it rhymed," recalled Léonie. "Nonetheless he faithfully left his poems on my pillow at night and all of them were just precious. I just wish I had saved them." It would seem that Léonie was a lady who frequently inspired men to write poetry!

On a later occasion, Bing became very sick; he was coughing frequently and Léonie feared he might have tuberculosis. She advised him to go into Chinatown and seek medical treatment and also to simply have a rest. The Mays packed him up and drove him off to Chinatown, but the next day he telephoned the house and asked to come home because he was not happy there. The Mays, of course, took him back. "So he never did have a holiday," recalled Léonie with a laugh. But apparently he survived that illness.

Bing was also very versatile in the kitchen. One Christmas he produced a three-tiered cake in the shape of a pagoda for the family. It was duly photographed by Léonie and Gerald even took a home movie of it with his new movie camera. On another occasion, Léonie asked Bing to make a special dessert.

"What's name?" asked Bing.

"Well, Bing, it doesn't really matter what the name is," said Léonie. "You wouldn't understand it anyway."

"What's name?" insisted Bing again.

"Well, if you must know it is called Angels on Horseback," she replied.

Bing threw his head back and gave her a wave of his hand dismissively. "Ugh, me savvy. All same Jesus Christ!"

On another occasion, the Mays went out for an evening engagement and returned late to find a note pinned to the front door which read "Key under Mat" which would have welcomed any intended burglars. "We had such a laugh about that," Léonie said.

Léonie also recalled a younger Chinese gardener who was diabetic and sadly had to leave their employ. Three of their Chinese cooks each stayed with them at least thirteen years, living in the accommodation over the garage. The old Pichon log cabin became a caretaker's cottage while the Mays were in England from 1935 to 1939 for their children's education and continued in this use for many years.

Aside from the caretaker, no servants were required while the family was away. When they returned in 1939 they were not able to secure a new cook right away, forcing Léonie to fall back on her Roedean cooking instruction days. The results of this new foray into domesticity were mixed at best, though her grandson recalls she was a very good cook when he was old enough to remember and appreciate her cooking. Léonie herself recalled to him that she and her daughter Moira would save up their sugar ration cards during the war years in order to bake a cake. On the day they finally had enough sugar to proceed, the cake was prepared and put into the oven. "It came out so hard and flat that it was completely inedible," said Léonie. "We were so ashamed of it that we took it out and buried it in the garden!"

Tom and Chew were the last Chinese servants employed at the house and were still there during the 1940s and well into the late 1950s by which time lifestyles had changed considerably. It was no longer the same world of upper and lower class. Throughout the early years, however, there were always servants, maids and housekeepers who lived in quarters in the attic on the fourth

Above: Tom, a cook for the Mays, shown in 1939.

Servants often did double duty, as shown here with Bing mowing the lawn in his cook's clothing.

floor, accessed by the second servants' staircase in the house.

The Mays also hired nannies through the years to take care of their three children. The first, according to photographs, appears to have been a lady named Brownie. Another was a Miss Muckle who locked their daughter Moira in a closet one day for misbehaving. Léonie was so annoyed with her that she fired her on the spot.

As Léonie recalled, "It was a totally different world back then. I still have a strong memory of listening on occasion to the Chinese gardeners arguing violently in Cantonese over a gardening issue they disagreed on...but they were all such good, faithful people who took great care of us. We loved them all."

It was indeed a very different world at Dunmora in those early years, depicted vividly through Léonie's photographs and through memories she passed on to her grandchildren.

Summers were always pleasantly spent down by the beach or on the lawns as the Mays hosted many badminton and tennis parties with friends. A wooden tennis court had been built on the grounds in the mid-1920s, only the second wooden court in the area. The first was built by the Birleys, a notable building

The original wooden tennis court in 1927.

The greenhouse at Dunmora.

construction family who also lived on the peninsula. (The firm later designed New Dunmora and the *Times Colonist* building in Victoria.) The boards on the Birley tennis court were laid sideways whereas the Mays laid theirs lengthwise which made it better for bouncing the ball. The Mays' court remained for many years and was still there in the early 1980s, though badly decayed and overgrown. It was then replaced with a hard court and eventually removed all together when the property was subdivided in 2012.

In June 1926, a rockery was planted at both ends of the veranda, complete with a sundial, and a rose garden was started. Léonie especially enjoyed her herbaceous borders of dahlias, petunias and begonias, which the gardeners always kept in immaculate order.

Sometime in 1929, Gerald May, with his civil engineering expertise, designed a bridge and boardwalk to make access to the beach much easier. Léonie described the long trek down there as about a ten-minute walk. In the early days, whenever the family went for a picnic on the beach her son Ian recalled she very often forgot something back at the house and would say, "Ian, be a darling and run back up and fetch…" whatever it was she had forgotten. It was a long hike back up nearly one hundred feet above sea to the house for poor little Ian.

The terrace under construction in 1931

In early 1931 the Mays decided to have a terrace built up with a large retaining wall so that the land would be more level. In order to make this happen, a small-scale railway line (nicknamed by Léonie "a miniature CPR") was constructed in order to carry materials of all kinds. The excavations behind the house produced soil and rubble for fill as well as granite for the retaining wall and stairs.

The garden pool at Dunmora was also built at this time. The fountain which is now a prominent feature in the centre was an addition installed by a later owner.

In 1934, the Mays built a second large reservoir on the property thirty feet in diameter to increase the water supply and pressure in the house. During the curing process, a man was employed to tend a fire inside it all through the night.

By the 1930s, perhaps because of Gerald's membership at the famous Union Club in Victoria, the Mays had a large circle of friends and hosted many parties. One friend in particular was Cecil Henry Meares, a man of many talents. His career had covered years of military service, fur trading, and acting as the chief dog handler for Robert Falcon Scott on the Terra

Church Bazaar on lawn, 1934.

Nova Expedition to Antarctica between 1910 and 1913. An Irishman by birth, Meares enjoyed having fun and travelling the globe and was said to dislike following orders. In later life he retired to Victoria and took great delight in visiting Dunmora and sitting on the terrace overlooking the inlet. He died in 1937 and, at his request, his ashes were spread in one of Léonie's rockery gardens beneath the terrace so that he would continue to enjoy that spectacular view throughout eternity.

The Mays also held one or two church bazaars for nearby St. Stephen's Church. "We were not really churchy people," claimed Léonie, "but we enjoyed the bazaars and helped where we could." These bazaars were organized by the St. Stephen's Woman's Auxiliary and people were bussed out from Victoria to the beautiful gardens of Dunmora in order to buy home cooking and enjoy the surroundings while tea and ice cream were served.

Not surprisingly, during the building of Dunmora and the later depression years the Mays began to run out of money. Gerald's sister Vera, who had been wise and very thrifty with her initial inheritance, often helped them out, a fact confirmed in Gerald May's ledgers.

Peter and Ian May playing in the new pond with Gerald May looking on, July 1931.

During the 1930s, according to the photographic collection, there were stables at Dunmora and a 1932 picture shows Moira astride her horse, Bruce. A very elaborate greenhouse was also built, which supplied the family with fresh produce.

The Mays also acquired many different cars through the years. Another grandson, Michael (one of Peter May's sons), has kept three of those vintage May cars in the family. He recalls the original "Sally" a McLoughlin Buick roadster purchased by his grandparents in 1932 and the "Sally Ann" Buick from the early 1920s which preceded it. When the Sally was still quite new they had it shipped to Banff so that they could drive it through Western Canada.

In 1982, Michael May, a car enthusiast himself, managed to find the 1932 roadster and prevailed upon the owner, Jack Shepherd, to bring it down to Victoria from Prince Rupert so that Léonie could see it again. In return, she agreed to return the original shiny metal trunk that had always graced its back bumper. Shepherd was thrilled and when he later became frail, he offered the car to Michal who agreed to purchase it back into the family.

Moira on her horse "Bruce" in March, 1939.

The Mays also owned an old 1920s truck, named Susie, which served as a work vehicle for Gerald around the estate. Susie was later replaced with a blue 1941 Dodge pick-up truck, and finally in 1958 by a fire-engine-red Wille Dodge Jeep, complete with an A-frame boom, winch, dump trailer and snow plough. The grandchildren later learned to drive on this vehicle out at the Dunmora estate, and it was Léonie herself who taught her grandchildren to drive it. More than a few Christmas trees growing in the former horse pasture fell victim to those efforts! In 1966, the Jeep passed to Ian who kept it as a work vehicle on his properties until 2001 when he gave it to Michael. It is now fully restored as part of Michael's collection of cars.

Another friend of Gerald's was Norman Yarrow who headed up Victoria Yarrow Shipyards at the time. His father was Sir Alfred Yarrow, founder of the renowned Yarrows Shipbuilders on the River Clyde in Scotland. Norman would often drive out to Dunmora in his 1930 Packard Touring Car which he had purchased from Plimley Motors for the sum of $10,000, an enormous amount of money at the start of the Depression. He sold the Packard in 1938 and apparently the next owner allowed it to be used by King George VI and Queen Elizabeth on their visit to Victoria in 1939.

Norman's grandson Chris Yarrow, another vintage car enthusiast, spent many years tracing the car's

Michael May shown with 'Sally,' a McLoughlin Buick roadster, in 2016.

owners, hoping to return it to the family one day. He was finally able to do this in 1985 when he purchased it back for the sum of $70,000. By then it was in need of a complete restoration. He was running an airline in the Northwest Territories at the time, but during those years the car sat waiting for his return, taken care of by his friend Michael May. Chris returned to Victoria in 2010 and restoration work began in earnest with the original leather interiors and fenders changed from black to chocolate brown and the exterior painted a bright yellow. Its value today is said to be around $250,000.

Trevor May borrowed the Packard for his wedding on May 17, 2015, to Violet Leclaire (nee Bartlett). The bride and groom posed with the car outside Dunmora alongside the port-cochére, where it had been parked on so many occasions when Norman Yarrow visited his friends there so long ago.

As their three children grew older, Gerald and Léonie decided they should be educated in England, so between 1935 and 1939 much of their time was spent in the United Kingdom. Gerald's ledgers show considerable expenditure at places like Selfridges and Harrods in London for school supplies, in addition to

Trevor May borrowed this 1930 Packard Touring Car, which Michael May cared for after its restoration, for his 2015 wedding.

extensive travel expenditures back and forth and hotel billing. The family rented a flat on the Ramslade Estate in Kent and spent some of their holidays on the Norfolk Broads while staying in the UK. Ian May was ten and Peter eleven when they left and both attended Stone House Preparatory School in Kent, and Peter later attended a school in Stowe. Moira, who was thirteen, apparently intensely disliked the school chosen for her.

In addition to all these extra expenses, Dunmora had to be maintained in their absence. They had left a gardener named Mann, the first non-Chinese gardener they had ever hired, in charge of the grounds. Ledgers show wages being paid to an E.J. Mann and a J.T. Mann so they might well have been a father/son team. Upon their return, Mr. Mann had a habit of trailing behind Léonie when she wandered through her greenhouse to pick flowers for the house. Every time she selected some for picking, Mann would say, "Oh yes, you can cut those but not those..." Léonie was somewhat indignant that he should presume to have ownership over her flowers, perhaps not fully understanding the gardener's natural pride while he had acted as her steward in her absence.

By 1939, the rumblings of war in Europe were being felt and Gerald decided he should send his wife and children home. He sold up much of his business interests in England and Léonie and the children were sent back to Canada aboard a Danish ship. Their schooling then took place at Brentwood College, St. Margaret's School, and Royal Roads, until Peter and Moira both became old enough to serve their country.

Life was definitely changing for the May family as the war got underway in Europe in all its fury.

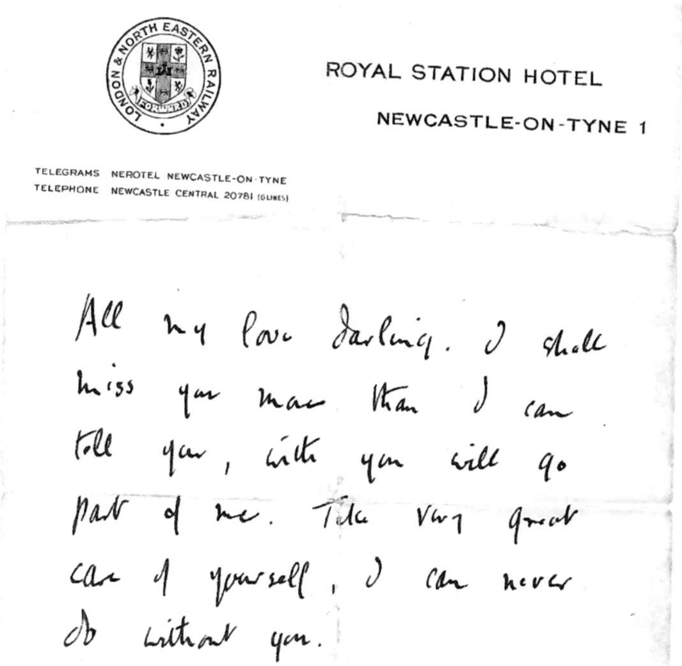

LONDON & NORTH EASTERN RAILWAY

ROYAL STATION HOTEL

NEWCASTLE-ON-TYNE 1

TELEGRAMS NEROTEL NEWCASTLE-ON-TYNE
TELEPHONE NEWCASTLE CENTRAL 20781 (6 LINES)

All my love darling. I shall miss you more than I can tell you, with you will go part of me. Take very great care of yourself, I can never do without you.

Gerald's letter to his wife as he sent her back to Canada when war broke out in 1939.

Gerald and Léonie by the water in Summer 1937 when they came back from England for a bit.

Ian in the pond.

The two boys at the IMP hut in Spring, 1935.

Chapter 4: The Later May Years (1939–1961)

The War and all that came after

Having made sure his wife and children were safely home at Dunmora, Gerald also returned to Canada in November 1939. England was certainly no longer considered a safe place after war had been officially declared in September of that year.

Life at Dunmora was somewhat removed from all that was happening in Europe. Léonie soon set about making improvements to the house by remodelling the master bedroom in 1940 and refurnishing the sunroom. The Chinese servants often undertook different duties for the family during the late 1930s and early 1940s. A photograph shows Bing, for example, mowing the lawn (a gardener's job) in his cook's uniform. A later photograph shows Léonie and Moira preparing a meal themselves in the kitchen, without the help of staff!

However, by 1942 the war, which it had been thought would be over within a year, was continuing and beginning to affect the family in many ways. Léonie's father, Rex, who had moved to Canada in 1922 and lived with his wife near Dunmora, was briefly kept under surveillance by the RCMP because of his German heritage. It is believed this surveillance included monitoring his mail and his movements, even though he was a naturalized Canadian citizen and patriotic to the cause.

Meanwhile, Gerald signed up as a local volunteer and was issued with a firearm for home guard duty in Canada.

By then, son Peter was a naval cadet at Royal Roads Military Academy and was called up in August of

From left: Ian, Moira, Peter's wife Marjorie, and Peter.

1943. He served as Midshipman P.G. May on HMS Belfast and in December that year was involved in the Battle of North Cape at which the Belfast assisted in the destruction of the German warship Scharnhorst. In June of 1944, the Belfast took part in Operation Overlord, which helped support the Normandy landings. In June of the following year the Belfast was redeployed to the Far East to join the British Pacific Fleet, arriving shortly before the end of World War II.

Moira May left home in September 1944 to train as a nurse and St. John's Ambulance Brigade driver in London (S.J.A.B.) and in 1945 she was posted to Bangalore, India. These were worrying times for Gerald and Léonie with two of their children serving overseas. They hoped that war would be over well before their youngest, Ian, would also be old enough to join up.

The Mays also entertained the Lord Mayor of London at Dunmora during the war and apparently had even offered refuge for him and his family. The Lord Mayor was said to be grateful but graciously declined their offer, feeling he should remain in London at this crucial time.

Nonetheless, the Mays still managed to enjoy their tranquil life by the water for boating expeditions. Fishing was especially prominent in their lives and there are many photographs of their fishing trips and the family boats: the *Moira*, *Moira II* and *Gypsy*. There are also many photographs of their many dogs (such as Chips and Cocoa) that were all obviously adored.

But life was definitely very different now. The halcyon, carefree days of the early Dunmora years were no more.

On April 24, 1944, their faithful servant Bing left after ten years of service to the family in order to work for a Mrs. Goulden. Sadly, they later learned that Bing had committed suicide by hanging himself. It was a tragic end to a devoted and trustworthy man.

The war continued and in May 1945 another friend of Gerald May's, Flight Lieutenant Alec George

Moira May left home in September, 1944 to train as a nurse.

On April 24, 1944, Bing left after ten years of service to the family to work for a Mrs. Goulden.

Gardner-Medwin, spent some time at Dunmora in order to conduct practice bombing drills over the inlet. The previous September, Alec had been awarded the Distinguished Flying Cross for bravery after completing twenty-seven sorties over heavily defended targets in Germany and Italy. Now stationed at Pat Bay and before his retirement in September 1945, he was experimenting with new bombing skills for future pilots.

A friend of Gerald May's, Flight Lieutenant Alec George Gardner-Medwin, spent some time at Dunmora to conduct practice bombing drills over the inlet.

Gerald and Léonie accompanied Alec down to the look-out on their property to watch these drills taking place over the waters of the Saanich Inlet and listened in to the interaction between Alec Medwin and his pilots. Léonie was later quoted as innocently wondering why all the pilots were named "Roger." Fortunately, those particular bombing drills were never put into practice because the war ended soon after.

At the end of the war Moira met Englishman Alan Statham in India and they were married in Singapore. They settled in Yorkshire but eventually moved

Family activities by the boat ramp – Ian at left with child on his lap and Gerald standing to right. Others are friends.

to Canada in the late 1960s. They had two sons, Gary and Chris, who still reside in British Columbia.

In 1946 Peter married Marjorie Beech. They had two sons, Michael and Rodney, and a daughter, Alannah, born in Halifax, who was a "blue baby" and not expected to survive birth. However, she surprised everyone and did survive for many years. She was a bright young woman and went on to become a teacher and later pursue her vocation to become a nun in Philadelphia. She eventually moved to France where her heart became weaker and she needed surgery. Having achieved all she wanted to do in life, she decided to risk surgery and have a heart transplant. Sadly, she died from complications of the surgery in Paris in 1984 at the young age of thirty-five.

Ian married Brenda Elise Boag and they had one son, Trevor, in 1966, and one daughter, Wendy, in 1968. Today, Ian, at age ninety-one, is the only surviving son of Gerald and Léonie.

Léonie died in September 1998 at the age of ninety-eight. Peter died two months later aged seventy-four. Moira died after a year-long illness with cancer in September of 2011.

Christmas dinner in dining room in 1939/40.

In the summer of 1958 Peter and his family visited Dunmora from back east where they had been living. Son Michael was then eleven years old and vividly recalls fond memories of the final days with Chew, the cook, with his famous teas on the veranda bringing back the old lifestyle that had once been a large part of the Dunmora fabric for so many years. He also remembers one day riding with his grandfather, Gerald, in the 1949 Oldsmobile '98 down Dunmora's driveway at a rather high speed for a trip to Brentwood and nearly crashing into the television repair man! Later they returned to the house and Gerald was able to settle down to watch his favourite television show, *I Love Lucy.*

Sadly, however, the 1950s had also seen the declining health of Gerald May. In December of 1958, he had the first of several strokes which crippled one side of his body as well as his speech. By then he was nearly seventy-one and he and Léonie had already reluctantly decided that Dunmora was becoming too large and too expensive for them to maintain. They decided to sub-divide their sixty acres into two thirty-acre parcels; their plan was then to sell

Gerald and Léonie May on the upper balcony in 1944.

Dunmora and build a smaller version of their home (to be known as New Dunmora) on the adjacent property.

There were, however, still some legal issues to sort out including the release of an easement with their neighbour Mrs. Johnstone at Point Colville concerning a right of way leading down to the Pichon cabin. The easement went through the Point Colville acreage and had never been a problem between the two neighbours in the past. If, however, Dunmora was sold, this easement would have to be settled first.

This, and other legal problems, would prove to be very problematic for the Mays over the next two years. A tree-clearing company hired to clear the timber for the driveway of New Dunmora began to cut additional timber on the property and a court order had to be sought by Léonie to stop the loss of the forest land from further cutting. Her solicitors prevailed and the court order put an end to the fine print trickery.

Gerald in a chair reading.

Léonie with flowers – Lady of the Manor.

Chapter 5: The Battys and the Simpsons (1961–1969)

The first changes

From 1959 until 1961 the Mays had Dunmora on the market in an attempt to sell their home. The original asking price was $125,000.

Gerald's health became steadily worse and Léonie continued valiantly to sort out some of the many problems that frequently arose. Back on July 23, 1958, the District of Central Saanich had announced that they would only give approval to a subdivision plan of the thirty-acre parcel retained by the Mays if they would provide a thirty-foot road allowance from McPhail Road down to the beach for public access to the water.

Despite some further negotiations, it was another year before the Mays' lawyers were able to advise them that the subdivision would now be allowed in accordance with the Land Registry Act "without the necessity of granting access to the water to the Corporation of the District of Central Saanich."[8] The developers, Aldous & Salmon were then permitted to proceed with their subdivision plan.

However, on July 15, 1959 the Mays were informed by Central Saanich that council would not pass this original subdivision plan as submitted and it would

8 Letter to Mr. & Mrs. May from Pearlman & Lindholm, dated June 1, 1959. May Family Archives.

Dunmora is shown in the early 1960s with ivy growing along the walls.

need to be revised. All of these issues and delays were causing even more stress on Gerald's failing health.

At the same time, the Mays were trying to go ahead with building their smaller house New Dunmora nearby (it was still 6,000 square feet, only 4,000 square feet smaller than Dunmora!). It was designed by Patrick Birley of Birley & Wagg, Architects, and would be built by C.Q. Builders. It would eventually cost them $78,675 to build.

By December of 1960, much to their relief, they finally had buyers for Dunmora—a Mr. Arthur L. and Mrs. Mary H. Batty who came from Lethbridge, Alberta—but there were still numerous issues to sort out before the sale could be finalised on July 18, 1961, including the outstanding Release of the Easement through Mrs. Johnstone's property at Point Colville. This was finally released in October 1961.

The sale eventually went through at a price of $95,000 with the Mays still holding a mortgage on the house for $60,000, and the sale included all buildings, fixtures, rights and easements. Despite an agreement having finally been reached, their problems were far from over. They were, in fact, just beginning.

Upon completion of the sale, Mr. and Mrs. Batty decided to hold a liquidation sale of most of the interior and exterior fixtures that the Mays had included in the sale thinking they would naturally remain with the house. Although this was, of course, the Battys' right, their decision to sell so many items upset Léonie very much knowing that things such as lighting fixtures which had been so special and precious to them were being sold off and taken away from Dunmora. Many of those items are today most probably scattered throughout Victoria.

The Battys then proceeded to take the Mays to court on a number of issues which they deemed had not been fulfilled in the sale. These included so-called "misrepresentation" in the original brochure advertising the house and concerned the waterfront measurement which they deemed was inaccurate. In addition, they complained that the greenhouse was in a state of considerable disrepair, even though Léonie had already told them that it had not been functional since just after the war.

The respective lawyers for both sides were able to negotiate all these points and nothing came of the court proceedings. The Mays moved into New Dunmora in the spring of 1962. Three months later, Gerald May succumbed to another stroke and passed away in August. Léonie was devastated as she tried to rebuild her life without her beloved husband.

One happy event soon afterwards did manage to raise Léonie's spirits. It concerned her son, Peter, whose career in the navy had gone extremely well since the war. He had acted as commanding officer of the frigate HMCS St. Therese for three years, and then was commanding officer of the destroyer HMCS Yukon. One day Peter telephoned his mother from the destroyer telling her to look out of the window down the inlet towards Brentwood. There, sailing slowly up the inlet was the Yukon and Peter was standing on the starboard side waving up towards the house. Léonie experienced one of the proudest moments of her life as she watched her son commanding such an important vessel.

It also gradually became apparent that the Battys had not really wanted to move in and use Dunmora as their private home. In May 1962 they had applied to Central Saanich to rezone the property from agricultural to commercial use for the purpose of operating a private school for boys. It was true that in one of the original real estate brochures advertising Dunmora it had stated: "In addition to being an ideal family home, the property is suited for use as a club, resort, institution or school. It is in excellent condition throughout."[9]

Nonetheless, it seemed sad to the May family that the house which had meant so much to them might no longer be a family home. Living so close, Léonie still felt that she had a vested interest in the entire estate and had, in fact, retained some of the original use covenants over the property. However, the Battys' application for re-zoning was not approved so they rented the house out for awhile and, in 1963, they put it back on the market. A new family was about to move in.

9 Brochure "Saanichton, British Columbia" Preview Incorporated, The National Real Estate Clearing House, Los Angeles, Calif.

Agnes and Jack Simpson and their two sons, John and Peter, would be the next family to appreciate all that Dunmora had to offer. The Simpson family had previously owned acreage on Blenkinsop Road where Agnes had kept horses and dogs. They had later moved to Haro Road near the University of Victoria where they also kept sheep and dogs.

Agnes also loved the water, a passion she shared with her husband Jack and her two sons, and they spent many years cruising the waters off the BC coast. The waterfront location of Dunmora was, therefore, an ideal choice for the Simpson family, and Agnes could still keep her dogs on the acreage.

Agnes was born in Lee, Massachusetts, one of the six children of George W. Westinghouse III and Evelyn Brocklebank of Pennsylvania. Her grandfather, George Westinghouse, was an American inventor and industrialist who invented the railway air brake. He was a pioneer in the electrical industry, gaining his first patent for one of his many inventions at the age of twenty-two.

The Simpsons' reasons for buying Dunmora might well have been because of Agnes' ties to the Central Saanich area from when she was a child. The family lived in many other places—Washington State, California and Arizona—but when Agnes was only six years old her father had purchased Springwood, a house on Mount Newton Cross Road and members of the family continued to live in the area until the 1940s. Her parents had attended St. Stephen's Church regularly and are both buried there in the Westinghouse plot. The family was always very involved with St. Stephen's Church, and in 1950 they built the St. Stephen's Memorial Hall in memory of Agnes' mother.

Agnes and Jack Simpson never made mention of the Westinghouse connection and enjoyed a more simple outdoor life on their newly acquired property. As the house had been rented for a year prior to their occupation, it was in some disrepair when they moved in. There was also obvious evidence of various items having been removed. Holes in the walls showed where elegant sconces might once have been.

Upon moving in, one of the first things they did was to pave the long, narrow, gravel driveway leading up to Dunmora. The expense for this was shared with

Jack and Agnes Simpson

Léonie May who was still living next door at New Dunmora, where she remained until 1971.

The Simpsons also sold the old Pichon log cabin (which Mrs. May had allowed them to separate from Dunmora in the sale) to their friend, a Victoria lawyer named Robert (Bob) W. Chard. The log cabin then became known as the Chard cabin. Mr. Chard later tried to sell the cabin and its two-acre waterfront site for one million dollars—but was unsuccessful!

The two Simpson boys, John and Peter, loved living at Dunmora even though Peter recalls spending some years away at boarding school. But they spent the rest of the time at the house. Vintage features that still remained in the house, such as call buttons in the walls to summon servants from the kitchen or servants' quarters, were things that particularly appealed to the boys.

John, the older son by five years, boarded at Shawnigan Lake School from grades five through twelve. Peter boarded at Shawnigan for only two years (grades eight and nine) by which time his older brother had left. After the summer holidays were over in September, Peter would return on the

Brentwood Bay ferry. He remembers one September looking back towards Dunmora where he could clearly see lights coming from the window of the bedroom he shared with his brother. By using the venetian blinds, John was sending a message to him in Morse code. In typical brotherly competitive fashion, Peter sent a message back using his small flashlight. Suddenly the ferry captain leaned out his window and asked him what he was doing. The captain was more amused than annoyed by the boys' antics asking, "Would you like me to send a message back to your brother using the ferry's searchlight?" Peter readily agreed and all at once Dunmora and the surrounding landscape became a spectacle of brilliant light across the water.

A few days later, Peter received a letter from his brother in which he sarcastically complained that he could finally see again after being blinded by the light! He never attempted to send messages again.

When they turned sixteen, their father taught the Simpson boys to drive on the circular driveway around Dunmora. Peter Simpson recalled that he was not considered competent until he could completely and safely reverse around the entire circle with a trailer attached!

Both sons have happy summer memories spent in the grounds or down by the water at the look-out where they flew model aeroplanes. On one occasion they placed firecrackers in one model airplane, unaware that two fishermen were down below jigging for cod near the cliffs. When the fireworks exploded, both fishermen were very startled and took off in a hurry. Undoubtedly a few fish were also surprised.

At one time, the boys built tracks and a trestle for a small steam train and in the process managed to catch the grass on fire from leaking fuel. Fortunately, the grass fire was quickly put out. They built another smaller model train set in the attic, which was probably a far safer place for them to play. The Simpson brothers also recall building fibreglass model boats over the garage.

John also had an amateur weather station on the top floor of Dunmora. He recalled one afternoon when very heavy winds surged up the Saanich Inlet with speeds hitting sixty-five to seventy miles per hour (112 kph) causing a great deal of salt spray mist on

John Simpson's Datsun is shown in front of the Dunmora garage.

the house windows. John telephoned the Victoria Gonzales weather station with this information and they were very impressed as there was little or no wind at Gonzales.

In the spring of 1967 as a member of the Claremont School choir, Peter asked his parents if he might host a party at Dunmora for members of a visiting choir from Washington State. In all there would be approximately 130 teenagers visiting Victoria. Dunmora seemed the perfect location for such an event. His parents agreed, perhaps with some trepidation considering the large number of young people who would attend. A bus was rented to bring the teenagers out to the house from town. Other cars parked in the fields. Amazingly enough, the party went off in grand style and without a hitch.

For many years, both Agnes and Jack Simpson were active members of the Canadian Power and Sail Squadrons. Jack Simpson volunteered a great deal of his time to the Canadian Marine Rescue Association and was largely responsible for morphing together many individual rescue groups into what would become the Canadian Coast Guard Auxiliary (CCGA) and which has now become the Royal Canadian Marine Search and Rescue Association (RCMSAR). The RCMSAR only applies to British Columbia; it is still known as the CCGA in the rest of Canada.

During those years, the Simpsons hosted numerous Power Squadron parties at Dunmora. Like Jack Simpson, many of the squadron members enjoyed celestial navigation, so the guests often ended up star-gazing on the six-by-eight foot flat part of the roof. The access to the flat roof area was reached through a very narrow hatch from the attic, and Agnes Simpson often feared they would all fall off while looking up at the stars, especially after having had a few drinks! She suggested that it might be safer if they simply turned off all the house lights and remained on the ground.

Despite their love for the water and the beautiful setting of Dunmora, in 1969 the Simpsons decided to move to a smaller home on Ardmore Drive as the house had become too large for them to maintain. It was time for another owner to take possession.

Jack Simpson passed away in 1983 and Agnes in June of 2006. Three years before her death, Agnes was given a twenty-year lifetime membership award for her service to the Power Squadron. An RCMSAR rescue vessel she had earlier christened The Jack Simpson in memory of her husband is still active today.

The sale of Dunmora for the sum of $125,000 went to an Alberta couple and included a tractor and a jeep. Certainly by the standards of the day, neither the Mays nor the Simpsons made any money from their respective sales.

One day shortly before leaving Dunmora, Agnes Simpson recalled that a number of very luxurious black cars rolled up the driveway. Men wearing high-priced suits, dark glasses and looking like they belonged in the Mafia emerged from the cars. Agnes met them under the porte-cochére and asked them what they wanted. They said they would like permission to shoot a movie on the grounds of Dunmora using the house as a backdrop. The movie was to star Jack Nicholson and Karen Black and would be called Five Easy Pieces. The production company was scouting for a location with an elaborate estate and elegant mansion and Dunmora seemed to fit the bill. Agnes explained that the house had recently been sold and they would have to negotiate with the new owners.

It would seem that Dunmora had been discovered by Hollywood!

Chapter 6: The Cormie Years (1969–2002)

Politics and Hollywood come to Dunmora!

The new owners were Donald and Eivor Cormie from Edmonton, Alberta. Shortly before purchasing Dunmora, the Cormies had acquired the Point Colville house next door for a summer retreat for them and their eight children (John, Donald, Allison, James, Neil, Bruce, Eivor and Robert). When they returned to their home in Edmonton after purchasing Point Colville, their realtor telephoned them to say that the neighbouring property (Dunmora) was also on the market and asked if they were interested in buying it. He sent them some photos of Dunmora, knowing that the Cormies were already familiar with the surrounding area.

The Cormies immediately decided to purchase it, interior sight unseen, for the asking price of $125,000 with $25,000 as a down payment. When they finally came out to view their new home they were thrilled with both the style and the Tudor architecture. The Cormies owned many homes over the next three decades but Eivor Cormie always claimed that Dunmora was her favourite.

The Cormies also agreed to allow the filming of *Five Easy Pieces* to take place, but they stipulated that the production company should use their Point Colville house for the movie and not Dunmora. Jack Nicholson, however, was later invited for dinner at Dunmora and he was remembered by the family as being "very polite, interesting and funny." The family often went over to Point Colville to watch the filming and

Dunmora during the Cormie years.

Filming of *April Fool's Day* at Collessie

The crew relaxes during the filming of *April Fool's Day* at Collessie

Nicholson was one of many well-known people to grace the doors of the mansion in the coming years. *Five Easy Pieces* was released in 1971. More movies were filmed in and around the estate during the 1970s and 1980s.

One of the first things the Cormies did upon taking ownership of Dunmora was to change the name of the house to Collessie. This name came from Donald Cormie's Scottish roots. His grandfather had grown up in Collessie, Fife, and had immigrated to Fergus, Ontario, where he and a group of other Scotsmen had purchased land.

The name change from Dunmora to Collessie might not have been to Léonie May's liking, but she never mentioned it to her family and accepted the change in good faith. In fact, she became friends with the Cormie family who often invited her to the house in the early years when she still lived nearby. In any event, by the 1970s, the house was so well known as Dunmora that few people even knew a name change had taken place. The address was still simply 8100A McPhail Road, as by then New Dunmora next door had become Number 8100B.

Special effects staging during filming of *April Fool's Day* at Collessie

Filming of *April Fool's Day* at Collessie.

Donald Cormie had initially purchased the house in his name and then made arrangements for a family business, Estate Loan and Finance Company, to manage the property. The company name eventually transitioned into Gamal Management Ltd.

"Gamal was a Swedish name for home and was selected to honour my mom's Swedish roots as she was born in Eskilstuna, Sweden," said son Neil Cormie in 2016.[10]

Donald Cormie was born July 24, 1922, in Edmonton, Alberta. His father, George Cormie, owned and operated the North West Mill and Feed Plant known as the Ritchie Mill, which is now a famous historic site. Young Donald attended the University of Alberta from where he received his BA and LLB. From 1943–44 he was in the Merchant Marine, and after the war, in 1946, he obtained his LLM from Harvard Law School in Boston.

It was while in Boston that he met his future wife Eivor Ekstrom from Sweden. The young couple moved to Edmonton where Donald was called to the Alberta Bar and then worked for Smith, Clement, Parlee and Whitaker. In 1954, he co-founded the

10 Interview Neil Cormie, July 2016.

Donald and Eivor Cormie from Edmonton, Alberta.

law firm of Cormie & Kennedy. By the 1970s this had become the second largest law firm in Edmonton. Back in 1963, Donald also created the Cormie Ranch, which eventually grew into a 22,000 acre purebred cattle ranch near Tomahawk, Alberta. The family's primary residence was in the Grandview district of Edmonton. They also had a home at Cormie Ranch, in addition to their two McPhail Road houses and a fifth home in Phoenix, Arizona.

In 1953, while Don and a friend, Ralph Forester, who worked for the World Bank, were together at an Eskimo football game they had begun to discuss how they both believed in the practice of saving 10 percent of everything you earn for the purpose of investing. This discussion led to the two men starting an investment company based on this philosophy. This was the beginning of what was called the First Investors Company, a company that later developed into the Principal Group.

As an extremely busy lawyer and rancher, Donald Cormie frequently travelled back and forth from Alberta to British Columbia, with the family living in both provinces. Most summers, Eivor would bring the three youngest children to Collessie and the older children would come whenever they could, depending on where they were and what their schedules allowed. Donald flew out every Friday and flew back to Edmonton on Sunday night. The entire family, however, always spent Christmas together at Collessie.

Donald kept most items he needed to run his businesses at Collessie, but travelled frequently between Alberta and BC. Of Donald's many flights, son Neil Cormie recalled, "He would always bring a few incidentals and maybe a present in a brown paper bag when he flew in from Edmonton to Victoria on Air Canada or PWA (Pacific Western Airlines). The

The Cormie family renamed the house Collessie, the name of the Scottish town where Donald's grandfather grew up.

stewardesses got to know him well and remembered he always seemed to travel with a brown paper bag. One Christmas for fun all the children purchased a number of brown paper bags on which they had his initials DMC stencilled on the side (presumably to make them look a little more elegant). He was given this gift of bags with a card suggesting that "perhaps he could now travel with a little class."

During the summers, Donald drove out to BC in his wife's 1966 Gold Oldsmobile Toronado, a very stylish vehicle for the times, so that Eivor would have the car available to run errands. On one occasion she returned to the house with two of her children in her car to find another car parked under the porte-cochére with a young boy sitting in the passenger seat. The boy seemed to be very upset and told Mrs. Cormie that his dad had just picked him up from the ferry terminal and driven him there but had then gone inside leaving his son to wait for him.

Mrs. Cormie took her children inside, assuming that the visitor must be someone they knew. After searching throughout the house, she eventually found

Aerial view of Collessie, during the Cormie years.

a total stranger in the master bathroom where he had drawn a bath, removed all his clothes and was soaking in the tub. He seemed very agitated and extremely confused so Mrs. Cormie asked the children to call the police while she pulled up a chair beside the tub and started to talk to the man in an attempt to calm him down. By the time the police arrived he was considerably calmer.

She later learned that the boy, whose mother lived in Vancouver, was supposed to spend the weekend with his father. His father had indeed picked him up from the ferry but had a schizophrenic episode causing him to lose his bearings, ending up at the Cormie's house by mistake. The police took the man away for psychological evaluation while other members of the police force took care of the boy until his mother arrived to pick him up. This was just one more day in the life of the house!

During the 1970s, the house saw the comings and goings of many political figures, including Prime Minister Pierre Elliott Trudeau and his new bride, Margaret Sinclair Trudeau. On May 3, 1971, the newly married couple stayed at the house for a private getaway.

A friend of Donald Cormie's was a consultant to the prime minister and was very familiar with the privacy and isolation of Collessie. He thought it would also be an ideal location for meetings Trudeau would hold in the summer of that same year, so the Cormies graciously allowed their property to be used. Surrounded by forest, the house was a nicely kept secret from the public and the paparazzi. No one, in fact, ever knew that Trudeau was there June 14–16, 1971 for the latest constitutional conference meeting with the provincial premiers.

Several constitutional conferences had been held between 1968 and 1971, but the meeting in June 1971 was the one where the premiers drew up the document known as the Victoria Charter, a major constitutional review. The Victoria Charter was a package of changes to the Canadian Constitution with its key elements touching on fundamental freedoms and political rights, language rights, the composition of the Supreme Court of Canada, income security and a constitutional amending formula. Quebec Premier Robert Bourassa, however, announced that Quebec could not accept the terms and it became a

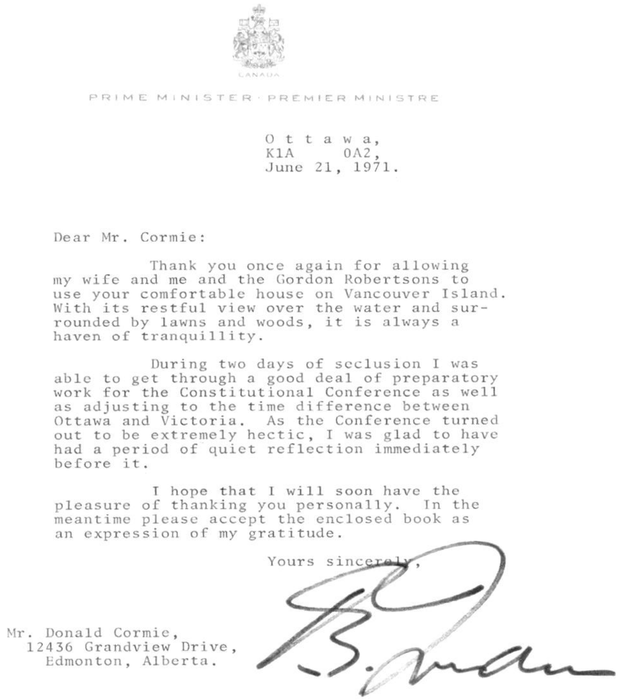

CANADA

PRIME MINISTER · PREMIER MINISTRE

Ottawa,
K1A 0A2,
June 21, 1971.

Dear Mr. Cormie:

Thank you once again for allowing my wife and me and the Gordon Robertsons to use your comfortable house on Vancouver Island. With its restful view over the water and surrounded by lawns and woods, it is always a haven of tranquillity.

During two days of seclusion I was able to get through a good deal of preparatory work for the Constitutional Conference as well as adjusting to the time difference between Ottawa and Victoria. As the Conference turned out to be extremely hectic, I was glad to have had a period of quiet reflection immediately before it.

I hope that I will soon have the pleasure of thanking you personally. In the meantime please accept the enclosed book as an expression of my gratitude.

Yours sincerely,

Mr. Donald Cormie,
12436 Grandview Drive,
Edmonton, Alberta.

Thank you letter from Prime Minister Pierre Elliott Trudeau who stayed at Collessie with his new bride, Margaret Sinclair Trudeau, in May, 1971.

stalemate. One of Trudeau's aides later told the Cormies that a compromise, which was eventually accepted, was drafted in the sun room of Collessie. Trudeau later sent a letter to the Cormies thanking them for their kind hospitality.

During Trudeau's visit there was, of course, an extremely heavy security presence. Many vehicles were parked along McPhail Road because the driveway to the house was far too narrow to accommodate them. At that time, Léonie May was still living next door at New Dunmora and the driveway was jointly shared until it branched off in two directions. She recalled that one night she had woken up in the early hours to see some flashlights in the trees between her house and old Dunmora. She knew that the prime minister was staying next door so she immediately telephoned the local Central Saanich police imagining that something suspicious might be going on in the grounds. The police rushed out only to find that the lights were coming from the security people who were constantly prowling the grounds to make sure nothing was amiss. In an over-zealous attempt to protect the prime minister, they were even taking down licence plate numbers of the cars belonging to Mrs. May which were parked in her own driveway. Eventually, everything was sorted out and peace reigned once again.

Son Neil Cormie recalled living full-time at Collessie in the early 1970s while attending the University of Victoria, at which time the house had a permanent staff of two. One of the housekeeping duties every morning was to "rake" the then very in-fashion yellow shag carpet throughout the house.

Neil's horses in the paddock at Collessie.

One of the Cormie daughters, Eivor, was the Alberta Junior Hunter Jumper champion one year and when she upgraded her horse, she gave her other horse to her brother Neil, which he kept in the stables at Collessie. Having been brought up in Alberta, Neil knew how to ride western-style, but did not know English-style, so he attended the Heaniad riding stables on Mount Newton X Road in order to train. Eventually he was able to ride in the local fox hunts and practise for a while with the local polo club. He recalls riding his horse regularly on the property and the horse would even walk up and down the brick stairs along the terrace in front of the house causing a number of bricks to become chipped. For the next decade, there were always horses kept on the estate.

Another Cormie daughter, Dr. Allison Cormie, attended many universities and at the University of Montpellier in France in the 1970s she had befriended Rashid Ghozali from Algeria. This led to a long-time friendship for the entire Cormie family with members of the Algerian Ghozali family. Rashid, a Harvard Business School graduate, was later offered a position at the Principal Group working for Donald Cormie.

Once Neil Cormie graduated from the University of Victoria, he moved to Milan, Italy to work for Banco Ambrosiano. At that time, the bank was planning an underwriting of an LNG project in Algeria for sales to France and Neil was sent to Algeria to undertake a report for the bank. He made a number of trips to Algeria and the large Ghozali family introduced him around Algeria. Rashid's brother, Djamei, was deputy minister of heavy industry. Another brother, Sid Ahmed, was head of the national oil company in Algeria and, for a time, was president of Algeria.

When members of the Ghozali family came to Canada, they would visit with the Cormies in Edmonton, but they all seemed to prefer socializing at the McPhail property due to its more relaxed atmosphere. Often the Ghozalis would bring other Algerian friends and there were many nights when the Cormies, the Ghozalis and associates would discuss the pros and cons of Algeria's LNG's projects while relaxing in the hot tub as the mist rose over the beautiful Saanich Inlet.

In addition to the Algerian contingent and their relatives and personal friends, there were also many other important visitors to the house during the 1970s and 1980s. There were visits from numerous Albertan and British Columbian judges and lawyers, such as Judge O'Bryne and Judge Bowen from Edmonton, Supreme Court Judge Willard Estey from Ontario, and lawyers Bill Baradino from Vancouver and Jack

Above: Dr. Allison Cormie in the 1970s with her friend Rashid Ghozali, a member of a prominent family from Algeria.

Kennedy from Edmonton. The father of politician Preston Manning from Edmonton was another guest as was Max Ward of Wardair.

Bill Pratt, the president of the OCO for the Calgary 1988 Winter Olympics, and his wife Millicent were also frequent visitors. During one of their visits in the early 1990s, Bill set up many different pieces of wood, all with different stains, in order to test durability for bench coverings. At the time he was head of the

Eivor Cormie and Peter Lougheed

Trans Canada Trail committee and was proposing to raise funds by selling naming rights for benches to be placed along the trail. He felt that the long Victoria summer days and rainy winters would be a good test of stain durability, so during each of his visits to Collessie, he would first check his wood samples left by the garage, before coming into the house.

Another good friend of Don Cormie's was Ken Marlin who was a major part of the Principal Group story. He spent a great deal of time at the McPhail property acting as a key player in all the conferences. Ken grew up in Saskatchewan where he worked for Canadian Pacific (CP) Rail, but Don Cormie recruited him for his sales department and from this a life-long connection was formed between the two friends.

Other visitors to Collessie included Peter Lougheed and his wife Jeanne. Lougheed was premier of Alberta from September 1971 until November 1985, and he and Don Cormie had been friends since their university days together at the University of Alberta.

The Cormies' eclectic group of friends also included artists Ted and Nicky Harrison from the Yukon and Canadian senator Grant Mitchell, as well as Victoria

musician/composer David Foster. For many years, the Cormie family was involved with the David Foster Foundation, which supports families with children in need of organ transplants across the country. Foster always held an annual Celebrity Softball Tournament to help the foundation raise funds and would bring in many celebrities to Victoria to participate in the tournament.

In the 1989 softball tournament, a group of those celebrities were invited for lunch at the Cormie house. They included such notables as Gordie Howe, Geoff and Russ Courtnall, Wayne Gretsky and his wife Janet Jones, actor Gene Hackman, Rick Hansen, actor Alan Thicke, skater Elizabeth Manley and businessman/agent Bruce Allen, to name but a few. They all enjoyed a pleasant lunch together on the grounds of Collessie.

During the lunch there was a heavy security presence. Two of the local security officers who had volunteered their time for the event went out towards the walkways along the ocean front. The hot tub and lookout was to the left and to the right was the walkway back up towards the tool shed alongside the garage. The officers followed the path down to the ocean where there was a ramp to the dock. At that time, however, the dock had not yet been installed and the ramp was winched up into the air to protect it from storms. The officers decided to walk out to the end of the gang plank, but unfortunately their combined weight was too much for the gang plank to bear and it snapped, sending both men into the ocean. Each officer had been carrying a hand-held VHF radio loaned by the police department for communication with other members of the security detail. Naturally both men were very embarrassed by the mishap as they had to face everyone after walking back up to the house soaking wet. At the end of the day, when all the loaned equipment was returned to the police, two missing radios were listed as "lost at sea."

Above: Gordie Howe and Russ Courtnall at a 1989 David Foster Foundation softball tournament lunch at Collessie.

The hot tub installed at Collessie had to be brought in by helicopter

Entrepreneur Jimmy Pattison of the Pattison Group was yet another friend of the Cormies. He and Donald Cormie were members of the World Business Council (WBC) and would often spend time together either at the Cormie ranch in Alberta or at the McPhail property with the Cormies.

During those years, Donald Cormie also held annual Principal Group planning conferences at the house. These consisted of a yearly sales conference and a yearly strategic planning conference. The law firm of Cormie, Kennedy also held its annual partners' meeting at the house. These many business meetings made neighbours think the house was only used for business. The Cormies always preferred their privacy, which merely added to this impression. However, during the summer months it was very much a family gathering place as well.

Grant Gislason of Vintage Hot Tubs in Victoria had installed a hot tub at Collessie, which was so large it had to be brought in by helicopter to be set out in the rocks far away from the house and overlooking the incredible view down the Saanich Inlet. It

The living room with shag carpet that needed to be 'raked' daily by staff.

was the first such hot tub at that time. It was made from old oak wine vats obtained from the winery on Quadra Street and still retained the scent of red wine wafting up from the wood. The vats were cut in half, benches were added and a heating system plumbed in. It soon became a special part of all the business meetings. Late night cocktails in the hot tub became legendary!

The planning conferences usually lasted about five days and all the employees either stayed at the Collessie house or at the Cormies' other house next door at Point Colville. In those days, two trails connected the two homes. One of the paths was a direct route down the hill to the Colville house and a gardener cleared a second, more scenic trail which meandered through the forest with a bridge over a creek. At one point along that trail there was a hollow in a tree with water from the stream trickling through the hole.

One year, one of the visiting children decided to have fun by placing a very realistic looking plaster human skull in the hollow, positioning it in such a fashion as to make it seem like it had just been unearthed by the water, and, over time, the skull tarnished from aging. Much later, someone wandering the trail noticed the skull and immediately called the police. Thinking this could have been a crime scene, the

The Cormie family always spent Christmas together at Collessie. The photo here shows the tradition in 1983.

police cordoned off the area and brought in the coroner to unearth the skull. As soon as it was lifted out they realized, of course, that it was a fake. The skull ended up on a Central Saanich police officer's desk as a memento, but Neil Cormie managed to retrieve it and place it back in the tree hollow. The following year it disappeared and was never seen again!

Donald Cormie's Principal Group, when still called First Investors Ltd., had initially used IBM computers; in fact they were one of the earliest companies to embrace computers. At that time they were so new in Edmonton that First Investors had the computer room on the main retail level of the IBM building fitted with glass windows to the street so that people passing by could stop and look inside.

During this period, a sales group from IBM attended one of the banking conferences at the McPhail property to pitch a new IBM main frame computer system. They identified the computer needs of the whole company based on each department's annual review

and future business projections. On the last day of the conference IBM presented the company with a new system for a growing company and gave a time line for how long it would take them to complete installation. It was a sweet deal, but First Investors decided that the new system would take far too long to install. One of First Investors IT managers suggested they should also contact the Geac computer company which had recently been founded in Markham, Ontario by Robert Isserstedt and R. Angus German. As a result, a lifetime business association formed between the Principal Group and Geac Computers. It was a wise move, as by 1976 Geac had broken all sales records and had become so sophisticated that it began offering its own online computer hardware. The Principal Group was using a system which was far ahead of the times and the attic at Collessie became the computer room for Donald Cormie's businesses.

Donald Cormie's law firm and investment company both continued to do well during the 1970s. One highlight of those years was a momentous and very special occasion for the Cormies. On July 3, 1973 Donald and his wife Eivor were invited to join the Trudeaus and Queen Elizabeth and the Duke of Edinburgh at an informal dinner party in Calgary. Donald Cormie often remarked about how very impressed he was by Her Majesty's detailed knowledge of all the commonwealth countries.

Meanwhile, the business meetings and conferences continued at Collessie during the winter months and the Cormie family enjoyed their summers on the property. The house was, however, expensive to maintain, so perhaps to offset expenses and taxes, Donald Cormie allowed more movies to be filmed in the grounds. These included *The Guardian, Back Fire, April Fool's Day,* and a one-hour episode of the then very popular TV *Love Boat* series. This particular episode, which guest starred actor Lorne Greene, shows him getting married in the grounds by the pool with a backdrop of the Saanich Inlet in one direction and the Tudor manor house in the other. Although it was

Above: Don Cormie making his famous Swedish pancakes.

The Cormie family by age in 1983.

supposed to be happening in Alaska, the location of Dunmora/Collessie is very obvious in that episode.

By the mid-1980s, the Principal Group had developed both nationally and internationally with offices across the country. Their computer system was second to none and allowed for real-time reporting. A principal trust financial centre did banking and, in addition, there was a dedicated sales force for mutual funds or fixed rate guaranteed investments. They were on the brink of receiving approval for property insurance sales and investment broker business offering one-stop financial shopping which, although is common today, was not offered by any other major financial institution back in the 1980s. Sales were up to one billion dollars a year and everything was on a roll.

Aside from being an important and well-known businessman, lawyer and financial adviser, Donald Cormie was also a philanthropist. Every year, he brought graduates from leading North American universities to work in fast-growing financial companies in Edmonton. Throughout his entire career, he was also a great supporter of Edmonton and the province of Alberta. He sponsored the 1978

Commonwealth Games and was the fund raising chairman for the 1983 Universiade held in Edmonton. From 1968–1971 he acted as a director of the Banff School of Management, was a director of Citadel Theatre (1968–1970), and was the founding member of the Business Advisory Council at the University of Alberta, as well as a supporter of the George M. Cormie Endowment at the Western Centre for Economic Research at the University of Alberta. In addition, he was president of the Canadian Bar Association (Alberta Branch) and a founding member of the Foundation for Legal Research. He was also instrumental in setting up the office of the Ombudsman for the Province of Alberta and was a member of the World Business Council, Young Presidents Organisation, Chief Executive Organisation and the Deans Council of 100 at the Arizona State University.[11]

Then, suddenly, in the mid-1980s there was a significant down-turn in Alberta's fortunes and this recession caused the financial bubble to burst. By 1987, First Investors, one of the many companies within the Principal Group, had foreclosed on a number of mortgages. Many local trust companies failed and the Alberta financial regulators undertook a review of First Investors, feeling they no longer had the required capital. The company argued that they did, stating that the government had not included the value of foreclosed assets which the company was still operating at a profit.

Nonetheless, on July 1, 1987, Dick Johnson, Alberta's treasurer, pulled the licences of First Investors so they could no longer sell new products. The Principal Group placed them under the Companies Credit Arrangement Act to hopefully wind them down in an orderly fashion. This, however, led to a run on the other financial businesses that, in turn, led to the Principal Group filing for bankruptcy. The government then set up the Code Inquiry to review the actions of Cormie's Principal Group and this inquiry focused criticism on the company officers, including the Cormie family, rather than the government's decision to pull the licences. This whole fiasco led to a five-year investigation by the RCMP and numerous law suits against the Cormies.

11 Obituary Notice – Donald Cormie, Edmonton Journal.

The 1999 Great Gatsby Party, one of several as the Cormie family said goodbye to the house.

It was a sad time for the Cormie family and they received much adverse media attention. But in May of 1994 the RCMP released a press report stating that after reviewing all the relevant material they would not recommend charges. The damage, however, had been done. After liquidators completed the winding up of the companies it was found that they were not, in fact, insolvent. In 2005, eighteen years after the licences were pulled, a settlement was finally reached with all parties ending all the outstanding actions and after paying the liquidator costs, the clients of First Investors received 99 percent back and CDIC kept the 39 million excess after winding up Principal Savings and Trust.[12]

12 Interview with Neil Cormie, July 2016.

For the next few years there was much uncertainty for both the McPhail houses. Collessie had always been a favourite home for the family. It was where they always spent Christmas together and they had grown to love the old world charm of the wood panelling, the formal entrance hall and dining room, the beautiful leaded glass windows and the buzzers which summoned the staff in the early years, reminiscent perhaps of a Downton Abbey era. They had relished the exquisite views down the Saanich Inlet and their memories of happy times spent with family and friends in the grounds and in the luxurious hot tub. The younger Cormie children, and later the grandchildren, had enjoyed endless summers on the water and the excitement of exploring the acreage.

The planning conferences and meetings held during the 1970s and 1980s were second to none and had developed an *esprit de corps* among all the participants. At one point, the Principal Group was listed by the Financial Post as one of the best companies for which to work.

Without the family business tying them together back in Edmonton, the entire Cormie family eventually spread to many different parts of the world, and by 2002 Collessie was no longer in use as the family gathering place for fun and relaxation. With knowledge that the house would be sold, the Cormies organized a few large parties to say farewell to the house that had meant so much to them. The first, in 1999, was a Great Gatsby Party and another, in 2000, was for a friend's birthday party, complete with live music, black tie and formal evening gowns. It was a fitting send off for the family.

By then, the outbuildings, kitchen and bathrooms of the house were all somewhat dated. The kitchen, in fact, had not been changed since the house was purchased in 1969 and by the year 2000 had come full circle and could be called retro. The house was finally put up for sale.

Don and Eivor Cormie moved to their home in Phoenix Arizona where Don passed away in 2010 at the age of eighty-seven and his wife two years later on September 13, 2012. Eivor Cormie in fact died peacefully in her sleep the same evening as their friend, Peter Lougheed, passed away in Calgary. For the family, this coincidence seemed to mark the end of all their Alberta connections.

Winter at Collessie.

It was time for another family to put its own stamp on the house and make its own memories at Dunmora, the house that had its name changed to Collessie for a few years, entertained the rich and the famous, served as the location for numerous movies, but, most important of all, had simply been a happy retreat for a family from Alberta.

Today, the name Collessie still lives on in a Cormie family property in Hawaii.

Chapter 7: The Greene Years (2002–2011)

Into the millennium

The next owners who purchased the house from the Cormies in 2002 were Valerie and David Greene. They came to Vancouver Island from San Francisco in September 2001 with a view to investing in real estate as seasonal residents, and initially bought property in the Uplands area of Victoria. Due to the exchange rate it was an opportune time to invest in real estate in Canada in general, and on Vancouver Island in particular.

After spending more and more of their time in Canada, the Greenes found that their Uplands home was becoming rather confining so they started looking around for larger properties in the Uplands area. In mid-2002, not seeing anything that fit their needs nearby, they took a drive out to see Collessie on the peninsula.

Like so many others before them, they immediately fell in love with the house and its surroundings and decided to buy it and move there. At the same time, they realized that it would need a great deal of tender loving care—and money—if they wanted to restore it to its former glory, because both the house itself and the grounds needed some work. Initially, they were both prepared to do this.

The Greenes had noticed that the name Dunmora was carved into one of the stone pillars at the driveway entrance so, suspecting that this was the original name of the house, they managed to trace Trevor May, Léonie and Gerald May's grandson,

Dunmora when the Greenes took over and before alterations to gardens.

The kitchen before, left, and after renovation by the Greene family.

who confirmed the name of the house was indeed Dunmora. The Greenes decided the house should return to its original name and Dunmora was born again.

In 2016, Valerie stated, "I would have been content to live at Dunmora for the rest of my life if things had worked out differently." Certainly back in 2002, she had most definitely felt it could become the ideal home for their family. Their two children, Jonathan and Madeline (then aged five and three), were also thrilled with the house and loved to play in the extensive grounds. David, a pension consultant, was willing to invest a fortune in Dunmora if need be. Together with their children and their two Pyrenees dogs, Bella and Marie, the Greenes were all set to make Dunmora a happy family home once again.

However, their list of repairs and necessary changes grew rapidly. The Greenes started by working on the garden, removing much overgrowth and rediscovering many wonders beneath, such as the sundial which had long since been covered over and forgotten. They were the ones who installed the fountain that still graces the garden pond, and put in concrete paths and rock walls. They then installed a rose garden alongside the sunroom. This vast maintenance of almost six acres of developed garden eventually required a full-time gardening team, which, at its peak, cost them approximately $10,000 every month.

Among the many garden and structural improvements was the rebuilding of an ocean lookout and part of a wooden walkway. They also had a two-storey, insulated tree house constructed for their children. This tree house still stands on the property today. The most pressing need for the house itself was a new roof, a job which cost them over $100,000. The original cedar roof, which for over eighty years had been known for its red colour due to the protective paint it had been coated with, was by then leaking badly. The new roof was a dark grey colour, made of the highest quality, synthetic shingles available.

In addition, the plumbing also needed a complete overhaul, as did the electrical wiring. The Greenes

Christmas party at Dunmora with Valerie, David, Jonathan, and Madeline Greene

remodelled the kitchen to their own taste, having custom cabinetry built to match the panelled living and dining rooms and leaded glass windows, and in an attempt to bring the house back to the 1920s period, Valerie began looking for vintage wallpaper prints to use in various rooms. The entire interior of the house was repainted in vintage hues as well, and every room was filled with beautiful antiques and expensive Persian rugs.

The attic rooms, which had been used for many purposes through the years from Chinese servants' and maids' quarters (May era) to high-tech office space (Cormie era), had become a storage area. The Greenes converted them into office space for themselves and a play area for their children. During this period, the Greenes' housekeeper told them there was a "friendly presence on this floor," and that some type of spirit had been sighted up there on several occasions. This was the first indication that a ghost might also be a resident of Dunmora.

The many improvements continued, including the addition of a guest room over the garage with a bathroom below, drilling a second well on the property to improve water pressure, and replacing the original boiler from the 1920s with two industrial Veissman boilers.

The Greenes also loved to entertain and held many parties, bringing in caterers and live bands to supply the musical entertainment. The walls were once again rocking at Dunmora! They held an elegant annual holiday party, a black tie affair with around fifty to sixty people in attendance. Birthday parties for the children were always carried out on a grand scale; the first was held on the lawn with a giant inflatable obstacle course and slide and a magician and clowns in attendance.

Eventually, however, the house simply developed into a "money pit" and the money began to run out. With the added expense of a mortgage and the annual taxes, it soon became virtually impossible to maintain.

In addition, the Greenes' marriage was floundering and by 2006 Valerie decided that she and the

Above: Wallpaper during the Greene years.

Back of the house with fountain installed during the Greene years.

children must move out to begin a new chapter in their lives. "I had to give up the two things I had put so much of my heart and soul into—my marriage and Dunmora—and it was the hardest decision of my life," she said.

It took another four years of marital litigation to enable the house to be sold. David Greene moved back to the States and Valerie also moved on, having by then purchased a home back in the Uplands with her new fiancée. In 2010, Valerie was finally able to remarry and now happily resides with her husband in the Gordon Point area of Victoria.

Treehouse built by the Greenes for their children.

Meanwhile, Dunmora sat waiting for the next episode in its life.

Chapter 8: Restoration of a Treasure (2010–2015)

More changes and upheavals

Towards the end of the 1990s, another young couple, Grant and Karen Rogers, had also briefly considered buying Dunmora. They even had it under contract but, after considerable thought, decided it would prove too large for their family. In addition, at that time there were still many liens outstanding on the property and Canada Revenue had become involved over outstanding tax issues.

The Rogers both loved the area, however, and as Point Colville next door was also for sale by the Cormies, they decided to buy that house instead. Grant, a land developer and entrepreneur, then set about demolishing the old Point Colville house and building a new one on the same footprint. A heritage consultant had informed Grant that the old house had nothing of heritage value worth saving because it had initially been shipped out west as a four-square Sears home catalogue home back in 1912.

However, once again the history of the two neighbouring houses would become intertwined, because by 2010 after the Greenes had left Dunmora, Grant Rogers decided to purchase the Dunmora acreage and the house itself. His plan was to restore the house and subdivide the surrounding land into eight two-and-a-half acre lots to be known as Dunmora Estates.

Back in the year 2000, after a high-paced, exciting, twelve-year career in high tech and fibre optics with

Dunmora after full renovation.

The renovation included new roofing with skylights to allow more light into attic spaces.

companies such as Seastar Optics, SDL and JDS Uniphase, Grant Rogers and his wife, Karen, had returned to the Saanich peninsula where they had both grown up. They decided it would be the best place to raise their family. In an article in Seaside Magazine, in 2011, Grant Rogers was asked how he would define success. He is quoted as saying, "Having a happy family and getting to do what you love every day."[13]

As a true entrepreneur, Rogers had started a new business known as the Marker Group in the early 2000s. He immediately saw many opportunities on the Sidney waterfront as being vital to the town's growth. Visualising a mixed-use development, in 2004 he began construction on The Residence at the Pier and the Sidney Pier Hotel which opened in the year 2007. The newly constructed building also included a grand aquarium and marine education centre known as the Shaw Ocean Discovery Centre.

13 Seaside Magazine, October 2011. "Can We Talk?" by Sue Hodgson.

The removation maintained the Arts and Crafts design.

This was only the beginning and many more exciting projects lay ahead for Grant Rogers and the Marker Group, including the development of the Dunmora Estates off McPhail Road and the restoration and complete renovation of Dunmora itself.

This was a challenge like no other. In an attempt to preserve Dunmora's past, Grant Rogers needed to also secure the house's future as a family home for generations to come. As an initial stipulation of sub-dividing the surrounding acreage, Rogers immediately entered into a Heritage Revitalization Agreement with the Central Saanich Municipality to apply for heritage designation for Dunmora.

The work began in June 2010 and Rogers was not surprised to discover from the building engineer that the house already met many of today's building standards. Paul Cosgrave, who was employed by Abstract Developments as the site superintendent, was also impressed with the workmanship of the house. "We did not encounter any problems as we worked with the heritage aspect of the home," he said. "We wanted to maintain that heritage aspect as much as possible. We needed to revitalize the house and at the

Ceilings were painted a lighter color and fixtures modernized, as shown here in the sunroom, where important meetings were held by former prime minister Trudeau and others.

same time give it the potential to provide the modern home owner with some of the niceties we outfit homes with today. At the same time we wanted to keep the original character of the existing home. I believe we did this very well and, to date, I regard this as one of the nicest properties I've worked on in my career."

Naturally, upgrades were still necessary in plumbing, electricity and insulation, and the porte-cochére needed revitalization. The seven original bedrooms were converted into five larger ones; ceilings were painted a lighter colour; and the kitchen was updated to an open plan with a mix of stained fir and cream-coloured cabinetry including built-ins and an eating bar. The front door entrance was altered to allow immediate access into the hall without the original inner entrance. An elevator was also installed, which would be an added selling feature for future purchasers with mobility issues.

Trevor May was disappointed that one particular light fixture on the staircase was removed and replaced by a modern newel post.

To enable all these changes to take place, especially the attention needed to restore the original fir doors, the wainscoting, beams, ceilings, fir floors and windows, Grant Rogers and his associates had compiled a dedicated team of exceptional craftsmen.

Original light fixtures were replaced with complementary period fixtures and paint colours throughout the house became warm and contemporary. Trevor May, however, was disappointed that one particular light fixture on the staircase was removed and replaced by a modern newel post.

The inglenook in the study was faced with granite, in keeping with the Arts and Crafts style. The large bedrooms on the second floor all retained ensuite bathrooms but were now updated to modern requirements by receiving the latest and best of new fixtures and fittings. The master suite, with its delightful sitting area, was decorated in a colour scheme very much in vogue during the 1920s. It still retains its original fireplace and has doors which lead to the balcony overlooking the Saanich Inlet.

Grant Rogers did not neglect the third floor or the basement either. The third-floor attic was converted into a media room with a bar and kitchenette for entertaining. Two skylights were added to provide extra lighting, as well as a steam shower in the bathroom. The basement level has now become home to an elaborate wine cellar.

"To take something such as Dunmora, with its wonderful heritage value, maintain that heritage and history and make it valuable for a new family to live in has given me considerable satisfaction,[14] stated Grant Rogers in an interview.

The house now awaited its next owners.

14 *Seaside Magazine,* February 2013, p.39.

The view from the entranceway.

The view back down the entranceway to the entry doors..

Exterior renovations capitalized on the majestic view.

The inglenook in the study faced with granite.

Chapter 9: The Zakreskis (2015–)

A million-dollar mansion

Dunmora, in its restored state, was now worth well over five million dollars, and after being on the market for awhile the house came to the attention of a couple from Calgary, Stephen (Steve) and Lera Zakreski. The Zakreskis had requested their real estate agent look for certain features in a house on Vancouver Island and Dunmora was put on the list even though it did not exactly meet their search criteria. It was pure chance that took them there, but from the moment they drove through the gates leading to the house they knew this was the house they wanted.

"I was deeply moved," said Steve in November 2016. "The house had the dignity of an old English estate and I immediately felt a spiritual connection to the property. The gates, the driveway, the landscaping, the house itself and its position in relation to the magnificent view down the Saanich Inlet, were all speaking to me. Within a minute of arriving, I started scheming about what I would need to do to own it, and I never stopped until I did. Yes, it was love at first sight."

Perhaps it was Steve Zakreski's background growing up in England which had instilled in him an early love for old English manor houses. He was born in Bournemouth, England, and was part of the post-war boomer generation. His parents were both displaced war refugees from Eastern Poland who had settled in England after the war rather than returning to the part of Poland which was occupied by the Soviet Union.

"England was very good to us," said Steve. "I have wonderful memories of the country and the people. They allowed my parents to stay and facilitated an engineering degree for my father who had served in

Steve and Lera Zakreski at Dunmora.

the Polish RAF, something for which our family is profoundly grateful. My father became an engineer in the aviation industry, and ended up moving to Canada as part of the Avro Arrow project. We settled in Toronto."

The Avro CF-105 Arrow was a delta-winged interceptor aircraft built by Avro Canada between 1957 and 1959 and was an advanced technical and aerodynamic achievement for Canadian aviation. It made its very first test flight on March 25, 1958, but unfortunately the plane was scrapped by the federal government a few months later in 1959. It still remains a controversial decision almost sixty years later.

Steve followed in his father's footsteps and also became an engineer and eventually a business owner, spending most of his professional life in Calgary. Coincidentally his wife was born and raised in the Ukraine in a town which is a mere one-hour drive from where Steve's parents had lived in Poland. Today, the Zakreskis have four children ranging in age from five to thirty-four.

Steve is the CEO of Southampton-Trane, a well-known air-conditioning company based in Calgary. He named his company Southampton-Trane because of his English background. When he was a child his family moved from Bournemouth to Southampton and Steve's memories of roaming the rural Hampshire countryside were all happy ones, so the name Southampton was included in his company's name. Initially he was not planning the name to be public but later the holding company became the working name for an active company and it already had brand recognition so it was too late to change—even if he had wanted to!

Calgary was very good to the Zakreskis, but Steve had always hankered for the sound of the ocean, foggy mornings, drizzle, mist, holly, greenery and the smell of earth.

"How could I not be attracted to Vancouver Island?" he said. "Ultimately the call of the ocean and a more temperate climate won us over."

The Zakreskis were not planning to move in immediately when they purchased Dunmora in May 2015, so they needed someone very special to watch over and take care of their house.

"We were exceedingly lucky," said Steve. "Marisa and Claude found us. They, too, were searching for a similar property on the peninsula of Vancouver Island and Dunmora was on their shortlist at some point. They had, however, just made a decision that they would build a new house instead and were looking for a place to call home during the construction process. They approached my realtor at precisely the point in time when we had decided to rent the property out while we were still based in Calgary. They have been wonderful tenants who seem to truly appreciate the magic of the property."

Currently the Zakreskis plan on moving into Dunmora in July 2017. As the main building is now a designated heritage building and has already been restored in an excellent way, there is a limit as to what they can do inside the house. They did, however, already hire Lemon Tree Interiors from Salem, Ontario, to do the interior design and furniture selection. Lemon Tree interacted wonderfully with Lera Zakreski and the result today speaks for itself.

They do also plan on improving the landscape. The gardens are already beautiful, but the Zakreskis have now partnered with talented landscapers to take the garden to the next level with an English garden theme.

Both the Zakreskis agree that they now own something very special. "We take seriously the responsibility of owning this property. Both the building and the surrounding landscape represent a creative work of art by a gifted architect and the original owners. They built an iconic property which represents a point in time when the British influences in the region were strong and those influences set the groundwork for what followed."

They see themselves as custodians of the property, which has both architectural and historical significance for the region and which will long outlive them. The property has already imprinted itself into the lives of the families who have lived and owned the property before them. The Zakreskis believe it will also play a significant role in their lives and the lives of their children and generations to come.

I am sure that Gerald and Léonie May would be delighted that their home is now in the ownership of such devoted and appreciative stewards.

Chapter 10: The Future

Stewards of a legacy

FOR ALMOST A century Dunmora has proudly stood overlooking the twenty-four kilmometer- (fifteen-mile-) long Saanich Inlet, a small body of salt water situated between the Saanich peninsula and the highlands of the Malahat on Vancouver Island, British Columbia.

With a maximum depth of 225 meters (738 feet), the inlet has for centuries been of immense importance as a fishery to both the Malahat and Saanich First Nations. Brentwood Bay, on the east side of the inlet and slightly to the south of Dunmora, is today home to a small ferry service which crosses the inlet over to Mill Bay.

An interesting feature dominating the view from Dunmora is the small Senanus Island (known also as Deadman's Island) located four kilometers from Bamberton on the Malahat side of the inlet. Senanus, meaning chest or torso, is a sacred burial ground and today is used by scientists for marine research. In fact, the entire Saanich Inlet has also become part of a scientific research area.

While pondering all these historic facts and the beauty and chequered history of Dunmora itself, one cannot help but wonder what lies ahead.

The two old stone pillars that once heralded the original driveway leading to Dunmora still stand on McPhail Road, but today they are barely visible, covered over with a profusion of ivy similar to the growth that once covered the house itself. Today

View from the terrace over the Saanich Inlet showing Senanus Island to the left..

Windows demonstrate the wonderful Arts and Crafts style of Dunmora.

this driveway only leads down a shorter pathway to New Dunmora. The pillars are situated slightly to the north of the new elegant pillars at the head of Dunmora Court Road, which leads to the newly developed Dunmora Estate subdivision.

Dunmora Court Road is still heavily treed on both sides and has retained the beauty of its long-distant past despite the appearance through the trees of new homes being built on the eight sub-divided lots. At the foot of Dunmora Court there is now a circular cul-de-sac, on the right of which are impressive wrought iron gates leading to the current shorter driveway heading up towards Dunmora. Meandering along that driveway towards the porte-cochére today, one might easily be reminded of another era when the vintage cars of the rich and famous during the 1920s and 1930s came to visit the family, or when later important personages arrived during the 1970s and 1980s.

The quarry used to create the terrace in front of the house was located on the opposite side of Dunmora behind the old greenhouse location. To this day, if

The cherry trees planted by the Mays still stand along the drive

you look carefully in that area you can still see some depressions in the ground where the May siblings once had made a fort, to which they often retreated whenever guests with other children were expected to arrive, the boys being notoriously shy. Further back, on the rocky outcrop behind the horse stable, Gerald May had built a play hut for his children which he called the IMP hut. During the 1970s, this old hut was rediscovered. By then it was decaying, so it was painted and a new roof put on enabling it to last at least another decade. It has since disappeared.

The circular driveway is still spectacular and full of grandeur, majesty and a touch of mystery. Many of the original cherry trees planted by the Mays around the circle still stand, but the exterior of the house looks slightly different to how it would have looked in the 1920s. The house also would have been reached from its original driveway, which had been paved jointly by the Mays and Simpsons in the 1960s. That driveway had branched off in two directions each leading to the two Dunmoras, old and new.

The interior of Dunmora today—restored and renovated to modern-day standards but still with an eye to the past—is an outstanding example of heritage restoration at its best. Dunmora's historical value has been preserved and protected to ensure its use for future generations. The challenge of preserving the past while securing the house as a family home for the future has been admirably met.

But, digging deeper into that almost century-old history, one might also pause to wonder what the walls would say today if only they could talk. Would they approve of all the changes? As you wander through Dunmora today, those walls still seem to speak to you of the past when servants scurried around at the touch of a bell to serve their employers with a devotion not found in today's world.

They might also speak of business affairs when conferences were held or dinner parties were catered for the rich and famous as they dined on fine china in the elegant dining room before strolling out onto the veranda with port and cigars to admire the view as the sun set over the inlet. Perhaps some of those people lingered in the comfortable sunroom to discuss important pieces of history, and maybe Hollywood executives and well-known movie stars planned other movies in those magnificent rooms.

Every heritage house is said to have a ghost and Dunmora is no exception. Through the years, visitors have claimed to have felt "a presence" in the attic on the fourth floor; one visitor even maintained they had seen a shadowy figure strolling on the veranda and then disappearing into thin air. Could it have been a gardener from the past? Or maybe Cecil Meares returns occasionally while his ashes have rested peacefully for decades beneath the veranda overlooking the inlet.

Two families, the Mays and the Cormies, owned the house for forty and thirty years respectively, so their lives certainly must have been embedded into the fabric of Dunmora. If, therefore, you tend to believe in ghostly presences, it is quite possible any member of those families would want to return and linger in the home they once loved. The ghost would undoubtedly be a happy one.

This would apply especially to Gerald May whose ashes were placed by Léonie on a rocky outcropping at nearby New Dunmora. After his death in 1962, she had risked climbing out onto the rocky overhang to place his ashes in a box in a safe spot where no one could ever disturb them. Michael May, her grandson, claims she must have had "the skill of a mountain goat" to climb out there at her then advanced age, but she was determined that throughout eternity her husband would rest overlooking the water and the beautiful view he had admired and been entranced by for so many happy years.

There have been many changes through the years, most of which have been duly recorded in this story as each new owner took over making an individual and unique contribution to Dunmora's evolution. Even the original Pichon log cabin down by the water's edge, which once stood alone on the acreage, has been party to name change and ownership. It still stands there today but has deteriorated considerably. Otters now make their home beneath it.

The walls of Dunmora might also echo with the voices of happy children through the years: Moira, Peter and Ian May and the May grandchildren; John and Peter Simpson; John, Donald, Allison, James, Neil, Bruce, Eivor and Robert Cormie and the Cormie grandchildren; and Jonathan and Madeline Greene. And perhaps this, above all else, confirms the fact that Dunmora was always meant to be a family home—just as Léonie and Gerald May had first envisioned it would be back in 1921. It is for future generations to maintain this legacy.

Last Words & Acknowledgements

It has been my absolute pleasure to research and write the story of Dunmora for the current owners, Stephen and Lera Zakreski.

It could most probably be called serendipity that first brought us together. The Zakreskis lived in Calgary and I live in Victoria, but they had read one of my books, *If These Walls Could Talk,* on heritage homes. They then discovered that one of the past owners of the house they had just purchased on the peninsula of Vancouver Island was called Valerie Greene (but spelt with an e). They wondered if it might be me, so they contacted me to ask if I would be interested in writing a book about the history of their newly purchased house.

I was, however, not the Valerie Greene who had once lived there. Nonetheless, I accepted the opportunity to write the story, not really thinking that there would be enough material about one house for a complete book. I was pleasantly surprised!

I would like to take this opportunity to thank the Zakreskis for offering me this interesting project on which to work. In addition, I acknowledge with gratitude the help and co-operation of Trevor May, grandson of Gerald and Léonie May. Trevor has been a veritable fountain of knowledge throughout. Another May grandson, Michael May, has also been generous with vintage car information and some family stories.

In addition, my thanks to Karen Burnett McLeod, the only great-granddaughter of D.W. Burnett, for information about the Burnett family who built Dunmora; Neil Cormie for extensive information on his family and the interesting visitors who came to Dunmora during the 1970s and 1980s; Peter and John Simpson for their Dunmora memories and anecdotes of life there during the 1960s; Grant Rogers for restoration expertise; caretaker Tim Herperger and restoration builder Paul Cosgrave; Valerie Foster for her

Dunmora at night.

advice and input during the Greene years; Marisa Christie for showing me Dunmora for the first time; my friend and fellow writer Joan Neudecker for her supportive input; Kami Norman for real estate expertise and Helen Edwards for digging out some useful research papers for me.

For the many delightful and varied photographs that enhance my text, I am especially grateful to Trevor May, Michael May, Peter and John Simpson, Neil Cormie, Valerie Foster and Jo-Ann Way of Nutty-Cake Photography. Thank you all.

Since thanks also to Hancock House Publishers for taking on this project and for editor Theresa Laviolette's expertise in improving the text.

Last, but by no means least, I thank my husband David who keeps the home front going while I write books and live my dream. Thank you all.

Finally, I should add that it is a known fact that everyone sees the past differently, and this is quite natural. It is especially true within families. For this reason, I apologize in advance if I have misinterpreted anything that the Dunmora families have kindly shared with me. I hope my understanding of their individual stories has made for an interesting read while, at the same time, I submit that there are indeed many truths. I trust I have adequately captured and described them all.

Valerie Green, 2017

Further Reading

Bell, Betty. 1982. *The Fair Land, Saanich.* Sono Nis Press, Victoria, BC.

Grant, Peter. 1998. *The History of Sidney.*Porthole Press, Victoria, BC.

Green, Valerie. 2001. *If These Walls Could Talk.* Touchwood Editions, Victoria, BC.

Green, Valerie. 2004. *If More Walls Could Talk.* Touchwood Editions, Victoria, BC.

Wilkey, Gwen & Michael. 1995. *Symbols of Faith: The History of St. Stephen's Church, Saanichton.* 1995. West Saanich Aero-Graphic Publications, Pat Bay, BC.

References & Research

Cole Harris. 2002. *Making Native Space: Colonialism, Resistance, and Reserves in British Columbia* (University of British Columbia Press, Vancouver, BC.)

Daily Pacific Commercial Advertiser, Honolulu, Oct. 17, 1884.

Love Boat Episode filmed at Dunmora.

Cormie Family Archives.

May Family Archives.

MacLeans Magazine.

Monday Magazine.

Seaside Magazine, Sidney, BC.

Times Colonist, Victoria, BC.

All Photographs courtesy of: May Family Archives, Simpson family, Cormie family Archives, Greene family, NuttyCake photography and Karen (Burnett) McLeod.

Index

About The Author:

B**ORN AND EDUCATED** in England, Valerie Green has a background in journalism and law and worked for a while at MI5 in London. She moved to Canada in 1968 where she met her future husband. They made their home in Victoria where they raised a son and a daughter.

Valerie continued a career in freelance writing as a columnist, feature writer and author of twenty non-fiction historical and true-crime books. Her debut novel (part of a family saga series) will also be published in 2017.

Her love of history in general and heritage houses in particular has been a constant throughout her life. Today, she is semi-retired and is enjoying watching her two grandsons grow up as she continues to indulge in her passion for writing.

Valerie Green